THE BEGINNING OF THE GOSPEL . . .

THE BEGINNING
OF THE GOSPEL . . .

Four Lectures on St Mark's Gospel

C. F. EVANS

Professor of New Testament Studies
at King's College, London

LONDON S·P·C·K 1968

*First published in 1968
by S.P.C.K.
Holy Trinity Church
Marylebone Road
London N.W.1*

*Made and printed in Great Britain by
The Talbot Press (S.P.C.K.), Saffron Walden, Essex*

SBN 281 02230 5

CONTENTS

ACKNOWLEDGEMENTS

Quotations from the Revised Standard Version of the Bible, copyrighted 1946 and 1952 by the Division of Christian Education of the National Council of the Churches of Christ in the United States of America, are used by permission.

Thanks are due to the following for permission to quote from copyright sources:

T. & T. Clark: *The Gospel History and its Transmission*, by F. C. Burkitt.

Cornell University Press: *Mysterious Revelation*, by T. A. Burkill.

FOREWORD

by the Master of Eliot College
University of Kent

No regular courses in Theology have so far been available for undergraduates in the University of Kent at Canterbury. This does not mean that Christian faith and questions about its basis have been dismissed as unimportant. It does mean that the University has looked in the first instance to the Chaplaincy to provide one important forum of discussion. The Chaplaincy was created as a joint organization sponsored by the Church of England, the Roman Catholic Church, and the Free Churches acting together, and the University has recognized and welcomed its contribution to the life of the academic community.

The lectures which form the substance of this book were delivered as "Chaplaincy Open Lectures" during the Lent Term 1967. They were intended to provide, for an audience not theologically trained, some Biblical teaching of a high academic standard. It was not supposed that those who came would have much Biblical scholarship behind them, and it was assumed that they would be willing to work by attending seminars between the lectures. The lectures were open to all members of the University and to the public. The response and the effect were encouraging.

Lectures of this character will be arranged annually. The audience on this first occasion was immensely grateful to Professor Evans, and the Chaplaincy cannot thank him sufficiently for starting the series so successfully. The publication of these lectures enables a wider audience to take advantage of the contribution to learning which they provide. It is a contribution which discloses, too, how Christian faith is clarified and strengthened by the discipline of biblical scholarship practised with rare grace and distinction in this study of St Mark's Gospel.

W. A. WHITEHOUSE

*Master of Eliot College
and Professor of Theology
in the University of Kent at Canterbury.*

May, 1967.

I

THE GOSPEL

In attempting to carry out my mandate I would wish to pay attention to the terms in which it was given. These were conveyed in the remark, "We want to begin at the beginning, and that means St Mark's Gospel". Behind that remark lies a story which, while it is familiar by now to many, will bear some repetition. It is a story of a great reversal with unforeseen consequences, and the story is not yet at an end.

Christians long ago became accustomed to the existence in the New Testament of four written works called "gospels", but it was not always so, and need not always be so; and it could be held, and has been held, to involve a contradiction in terms. For the word "gospel" in early Christian usage, and especially in the usage of St Paul to whom the word is largely confined in the New Testament, is a singular noun which does not admit of a plural. Other men than Christians, if they ever used the word at all, could talk of "gospels", that is, messages of deliverance, in the plural, since they might know a multiplicity of saviours, of whom the god Mithra might be one and the Emperor Augustus another; but Christians were Jewish monotheists, the gospel was God's gospel, and was by definition one as he is one. It was, therefore to be expected that if and when this gospel was put into written form it would be in a single authoritative version. But this is not what happened. By a process which we can no longer trace but can only guess at—because the churches by the end of the second century could themselves no longer trace it but only guess at it—four separate distinctive versions had established themselves as authoritative. To some this appeared improper, and attempts were made to reverse it. The heretic Marcion, who was perhaps the first to conceive the the idea of a New Testament at all, issued his (c.140?) in the form of a single gospel (apparently a revised version of St. Luke's) to accompany the epistles of his beloved Paul, who had always referred to "the gospel" in the singular. His contemporary Tatian, on returning to the East from Rome, issued what was called a Diatessaron, or single gospel narrative made up out of the four, and in this form it reigned supreme in the Assyrian churches for at least two centuries Neither of these two arrangements, however, prevailed, partly perhaps because the four did not lend themselves to successful harmonization, partly because each of the four had so established itself in some area, and with the backing of some influential church, that it could not be ousted. When in the desperate battle with heresy in the second half of the second century it was felt necessary to have a Christian scripture to appeal to, all four were included, and reasons were then produced, natural and mystical, why the single gospel should be quadriform. Eventually by force of ecclesiastical custom it became part of the nature of things that there should be four gospels, and that they should be the kind of books they are.

In this arrangement St Mark's Gospel came off badly. How else could it be? Almost all of what was in it was in the other gospels also, along with a great deal else besides which it had not got. There was a tradition, indeed, that it went back to St Peter, but even this was not sufficient to give it the *raison d'être* which St Matthew's Gospel had as the work (so it was supposed) of an apostle, and as supplying in model form the didactic material which the Church had come to expect from a gospel; or which St. Luke's Gospel had as the work (so it was supposed) of a companion of the Paul whose letters occupied such a large place in the Christian scripture; or which St John's Gospel had as the work (so it was supposed) of an apostle whose Christ spoke the language of that theology with which the Church was so

2

concerned in its doctrinal conflicts in the third and fourth centuries. We may illustrate from St Augustine. He saw that there was what fifteen centuries later was to be called "the synoptic problem", and he wrote (c.400) a book bearing on it, *Concerning the Agreement of the Evangelists*. He observed the close similarities between the first three gospels, and since, as with us all, his conclusions were to some extent already wrapped up in his presuppositions, and it did not occur to him even to question the then established presupposition that Matthew's was the first and original gospel, he came to the only possible conclusion on the evidence—that Mark had copied from Matthew. He speaks of him as Matthew's successor and, as it were, his lackey, and of Mark's Gospel as an abridgement of Matthew's, and this despite the fact that, whereas Mark's Gospel is as a whole considerably shorter than Matthew's, in almost every place where they tell the same story it is Mark's which is the longer and Matthew's the abridged version. There the matter rested for fourteen centuries.

In retrospect it might appear something of a miracle that Mark's Gospel survived at all during the first hundred years after its composition. At the end of this period its inclusion in the New Testament secured its survival from then on, but only as the most insignificant of the four, and hardly worth bothering about. Quotations from it are very rare in early Christian writers, and it was little used in the liturgical tradition, as can still be seen in the small part it plays in the selection of liturgical gospels in the Book of Common Prayer. A sixth century compiler, Victor of Antioch, could complain that he had been unable to find any instance of a commentary upon it. Because of this neglect its text remained comparatively untouched by the tendency in the Church to adapt a text for its own teaching purposes, although on the other hand its text was frequently assimilated to that of Matthew's Gospel as if to a superior norm. Mark's Gospel lived on, but it lived in the shadows; it was carried by the others.

The last quarter of the eighteenth century saw the beginnings of what we know as historical criticism, and so far as the New Testament is concerned it began with the printing of the first three gospels side by side in columns in what was called a "synopsis", and with the problem which then appears in all its clarity of the combination in them of great dissimilarities and the closest similarities. This is not the place to rehearse the to and fro, over a hundred years or so, of hypothesis and counter-hypothesis to account for these facts. The work is technical and detailed, and justice can only be done to it in technical and detailed books. Suffice it to say that there emerged as an almost universally agreed conclusion that Mark's Gospel was the original of the gospels, and that Matthew and Luke had relied heavily upon it for the composition of theirs. The basis of this conclusion was threefold: (*a*) that almost all of what was in Mark was to be found somewhere in the other two, whereas the contrary could not be said that most of what was in them was in Mark; (*b*) that the language common to all three more often bore a Markan stamp than the other way round, and (*c*) that in the order of events, when this was not identical, it was a case of one of the other two agreeing with Mark and not of the other two agreeing together against him. Lately voices have been raised against this conclusion. Both Dom C. Butler (*The Originality of St Matthew*) and W. R. Farmer (*The Synoptic Problem*) have been able to expose defects in the logic of some of the argumentation used, but without, in the judgement of most, succeeding in upsetting the conclusion itself, while the positions for which they themselves argue—for the priority of Matthew's Gospel in the first case and of Luke's in the second—are fraught with far greater difficulties than the supposition that Mark's Gospel is the common denominator of the other two, and that their use of it is the explanation of the agreements of all three together.

Here then was a great transformation scene. As with the turn of a kaleidoscope the whole picture suddenly looks different. Mark's Gospel came out of the shadows, and was thrown into sharp relief by the fierce light which now came to be played upon it. From being carried by the others it now appears as in

4

some measure carrying them. After centuries of neglect as the most insignificant of the gospels it now begins to take pride of place as a document in the study of Christian origins, and in this century it has received more attention by way of commentary and special study than perhaps any other New Testament book. But the priority of Mark's Gospel came to have further and unforeseen consequences, and it gave rise to a whole series of questions in a kind of chain reaction. It could now no longer simply be taken for granted as natural or as divinely decreed that there should be four gospels, or that there should be gospels at all, or even that we know what a gospel is. If the first three gospels were shown to be in a genetic relationship, then there were specific reasons for their writing connected with this relationship. Were other gospels written because the first, Mark's, turned out to be unsatisfactory, at least in some quarters? If so, why were their authors so dependent upon it? If Mark's Gospel is not an abridgement of something else, but other gospels an expansion of it, what was the explanation of that conciseness which had previously been taken to be abridgement? If Mark was the first to give early Christian traditions a continuous narrative sequence and to make them tell a connected story, why did he do it, and where did he get the idea from? Was it a shattering new departure, or was it so in line with what was happening already that not a ripple disturbed the surface of his church? Was he telling his readers, whoever they were, something new, or what was already familiar, and in either case for what reason? If he was the inventor of a new literary genre, what is that genre when looked at in its own right? If it proved congenial to the later Church only when modified by Matthew and Luke, what purpose was it intended to serve at the time of its writings? What is Mark's Gospel? What is any gospel?

These questions emerged only by degrees. They turned out to be questions which require for their answer whatever instruments of internal literary criticism could be devised, because such external evidence as might have answered them was lacking. The only early statement on the origin and nature of Mark's Gospel

5

is an isolated paragraph from an early second century Christian writer, Papias, which is preserved along with a paragraph from him about Matthew's Gospel by the fourth century Church historian, Eusebius. It says that an informant, "the elder", had told him that

> Mark, having been Peter's interpreter, wrote down accurately—not, however, in order—all that he remembered of the things either said or done by Christ. For he was neither a hearer nor a follower of the Lord, but a follower, as I have said, of Peter at a later time; and Peter delivered his instructions to meet the needs (of the moment), but with no attempt to give the Lord's words in any systematic arrangement. So that Mark was not wrong in thus writing down some things as he recollected them, for the one thing he was careful of was to omit nothing of what he had heard or to make a false statement.

The paragraph on Matthew runs, "Matthew drew up a compilation of the Lord's utterances in the Hebrew language, and each man translated (interpreted?) them as he was able". What is this information worth? In the opinion of some scholars it is worth nothing at all. Papias's statement about Matthew we know to be incorrect; is his statement about Mark more than guesswork? It is clearly made in defence of Mark, accounting the Gospel's lack of order a virtue since it had come from a slavish faithfulness to Peter's *ad hoc* manner of preaching. But if (as some hold) Mark's Gospel has a definite and sometimes subtle order of its own, Papias's statement becomes a justification of something which is not there. No modern scholar takes Papias's statement, as it stands, as an explanation of why the Gospel is the kind of book it is, and even those who make an attenuated use of it as indicating that Peter may lie somewhere behind some of Mark's material are seldom able to do so with confidence or effect. Since all later statements on the subject are repetitions of Papias with embroidery it would appear that our questions cannot be answered by recourse to external evidence. Nor is the tradition that Mark's was a Roman gospel strong. The latinisms in it are such as could be found almost anywhere in the universal Greek of the Roman Empire, and there is no sign of any knowledge of this Gospel in our earliest Christian document from Rome, the First Epistle of Clement, generally dated c.A.D.96.

We are thus driven back to the Gospel itself to attempt an assessment of it. How difficult this turns out to be is shown by the very wide variety of assessments which have been, and are still being, made. The most immediate result of the priority of Mark was what came to be called "the Markan hypothesis" and later "the Markan prejudice". This was the view that this Gospel, and this Gospel alone, is, and was intended to be, a straightforward narrative of events, relatively uncomplicated by doctrine, and possessing the self-consistency of a genuinely historical record. This view was nowhere better presented in English than in the third chapter of F. C. Burkitt's *The Gospel History and its Transmission* (1906). He concludes the chapter thus:

> I venture to think that what I have put before you goes far to vindicate the claim of the Gospel according to S. Mark to be a historical document, a document really in touch with the facts of history. . . . The other Gospels, even the Gospels according to Matthew and Luke, give us an interpretation of Jesus Christ's life. An interpretation may be helpful, illuminating, even inspired, but it remains an interpretation. The thing that actually occurred was the life which Jesus Christ lived, and our chief authority for the facts of that life is the Gospel according to Mark.

This view underlay the many lives of Jesus written in the nineteenth century and in the early part of this century; it lingers still in pulpit and classroom. The comment was later to be made on it that one of the first results of the priority of Mark's Gospel was that that Gospel was appreciated for precisely the wrong reason.

The Markan hypothesis was undermined from two sides, the doctrinal and the literary-critical. From the doctrinal side came in 1901 Wilhelm Wrede's book *Das Messiasgeheimnis in den*

Evangelien (*The Messianic Secret in the Gospels*), in which the point was made that a constituent element in the gospels, and particularly in Mark's Gospel, is the mystery and secrecy introduced into the story by Jesus' injunctions to keep silent about miracles and about his messiahship, even in circumstances where the injunction could scarcely be obeyed. Wrede's own explanation of this phenomenon—that it was a literary device employed by the evangelist to account for the fact that the faith in Jesus' messiahship, born at the resurrection, had no place in the earliest tradition about him—was less important than that he had drawn attention to an artificial and doctrinal factor governing the story, which made it difficult to regard Mark's Gospel as an uncomplicated and straightforward narrative of events. From the literary-critical side came in 1919 K. L. Schmidt's *Der Rahmen der Geschichte Jesu* (*The Framework of the Story of Jesus*). This was a study of those passages which serve to link the separate stories in the Gospel together so as to make them a connected narrative, and Schmidt's conclusion was that these did not rest upon any tradition of a genuinely historical or chronological sequence of events, but are the construction of the evangelist himself, who often assembles his material on a topical basis of common subject matter. He summed up as follows: "In general there is no life of Jesus, no chronological sketch of the history of Jesus, but only individual stories, pericopae, which are put into a framework". These two positions, that the author himself is responsible for the framework of the narrative and for the punctuation of it by an element of mystery, constitute together the reverse of the Markan hypothesis.

What then of the individual stories? These were the concern of the next phase of gospel study known as form-criticism. This rested upon the assumption that the gospel material can, without doing violence to it, be separated out into paragraphs, each of which is a self-contained unit, carrying its point within itself without regard for anything which may come before or follow after. It is Mark's Gospel which particularly bears out this assumption. It has always been difficult, if not impossible, to detect whether Mark used any written sources in compiling his Gospel, but there is no doubt at all that no violence is needed to separate out its individual paragraphs. They come away easily from their present setting in the Gospel, and when away each is capable of standing on its own feet. The question then arises why Mark, as the originator of the gospel narrative, should choose to write in this curious anecdotal, stop-go manner. The most likely answer is that he had no choice, and that the traditions about Christ had already long assumed these fixed shapes in the course of being told and re-told in the service of the life and teaching and worship of the Christian communities. This is the most likely explanation, for even an alternative such as that of Dr A. M. Farrer (*A Study in St Mark*), who would ascribe more to Mark's inspiration as a writer, and to eye-witnesses, including St Peter, as his immediate sources, concedes that the reason for Mark's writing in this way is that this was the form which Christian tradition had assumed in his day—which, indeed, is implied by the fact that material in the Gospels of Matthew and Luke which is not taken from Mark often has a similar form. If this much is conceded it is a short step to say that Mark is not writing in imitation of something else, but is putting down in writing, perhaps for the first time, the traditional stories themselves

At this stage in the enquiry individual personal authorship is reduced to a minimum, and there is a high degree of anonymity in the material. The stories are often capable of being classified according to relatively stereotyped patterns which they follow. They resemble smoothed down stones, and leave the impression not of immediate transcripts at one remove only from the events, but of having passed through a number of hands before Mark used them, and of having left any individual eye-witnesses some way behind. If this is so, further questions suggest themselves. Why these particular stories, and what was their survival value? What function had they been performing in the interim? What in any case was a single paragraph able to do on its own? The form of the paragraphs may point towards answers. They are for the most part exceedingly compact and brief, devoid of any but essential detail, and so designed as to reach a climax quickly in something Jesus said or did. This is their sharp point, and it is when this point stands out sharply that they are in focus. The point is always a theological or religious point, bearing on Christian life. The stories are, as it were, on a circumference from which there is a radius to a common, though not necessarily identical, centre. Each is a gospel in miniature, and its context is the Christian message and life as the teller conceived that message and life to be. Already by its very selection as being particularly significant, and by the form in which it is cast to point this significance, a theological interpretation is being imparted to it. Further, since the stories were about something Jesus had done and said in the conditions of his earthly life, and the purpose for which they had been subsequently told had been to express a later and wider faith in him as the exalted heavenly Lord of the Church and of mankind, it is legitimate to ask whether in the telling they had become moulded to this later faith as expressions of it.

To study individual paragraphs in this way may be the furthest back we can go in the search for beginnings via Mark's Gospel. To be studying the Gospel itself as a whole is to be looking at the next stage in the development of the tradition, the stage of redaction. So far as we know, it was the first of its kind in the Church. Mark took the step of taking traditions which had hitherto lived and done their work as separate points on a circumference radially connected to some kind of common centre, and giving them a serial form in a straight line, in which together they constitute a single something, and tell a single story by continuous progression. But what is this something, and whence did Mark derive his order and pattern? Here within the limitations imposed by the early traditions of the churches gospel authorship is at a maximum. Unless we suppose that what Mark put down was all he knew, his attitude, like that of any author, will be involved in what he chooses from the material available, in the way he presents it, in the sequence and proportions he gives it. Here there is a further stage of interpretation. However he may be restricted by the fixed form of units of tradition, Mark's purpose in writing, and his understanding of Christianity, will appear in his view of the relation of parts to the whole, and of the whole of which they are now to be integral parts. Especially is an author's hand likely to be shown in how he chooses to begin and to end. How does Mark begin, and how does he end?

The beginning of the gospel of Jesus Christ, the Son of God. As it is written in Isaiah the prophet,
"Behold, I send my messenger before thy face,
who shall prepare thy way;
the voice of one crying in the wilderness:
Prepare the way of the Lord,
make his paths straight—"
John the baptizer appeared in the wilderness, preaching a baptism of repentance for the forgiveness of sins. And there went out to him all the country of Judea, and all the people of Jerusalem; and they were baptized by him in the river Jordan, confessing their sins. Now John was clothed with camel's hair, and had a leather girdle around his waist, and ate locusts and wild honey. And he preached saying, "After me comes he who is mightier than I, the thong of whose sandals I am not worthy to stoop down and untie. I have baptized you with water; but he will baptize you with the Holy Spirit".

In those days Jesus came from Nazareth of Galilee and was baptized by John in the Jordan. And when he came up out of the water, immediately he saw the heavens opened and the Spirit descending upon him like a dove; and a voice came from heaven, "Thou art my beloved Son; with thee I am well pleased".

The Spirit immediately drove him out into the wilderness. And he was in the wilderness forty days tempted by Satan; and he was with the wild beasts; and the angels ministered to him.

Now after John was arrested, Jesus came into Galilee, preaching the gospel of God, and saying, "The time is fulfilled, and the kingdom of God is at hand; repent, and believe in the gospel" (R.S.V.).

It is generally agreed that these sentences belong together in that they are not a beginning in the sense of opening incidents

11

in a narrative, but are a prelude to, and presupposition of, the narrative proper which begins with the call of disciples, and to which the verses describing Jesus' entry into Galilee and giving a summary of his message are a transition. Immediately striking about this prelude, as a whole and in its parts, is an extreme brevity and compression, almost at times to the point of unintelligibility. Thus it is not clear how the first four verses are to be punctuated and hence construed—the differences of punctuation may be seen in the various English versions. Are the opening words, "The beginning of the gospel of Jesus Christ" (the words "Son of God" are doubtful in the text) to be taken as a title of the whole work, which then begins with "As it is written in Isaiah the prophet. . . . John the baptizer was in the wilderness"? Or should it be "The beginning of the gospel of Jesus was as it is written in Isaiah the prophet" etc., the story itself starting from "John the baptizer appeared in the wilderness. . . "? Or should it be "The beginning of the gospel of Jesus Christ was John the baptizer in the wilderness", with the Old Testament quotation thrown into parenthesis in between? It is further not clear whether by the "gospel of Jesus Christ" is to be understood the gospel which he preached, or the gospel which the Church was preaching about him, and the Old Testament quotation is a composite quotation from two sources, only one of which is Isaiah. Perhaps all this helped Augustine to his conclusion that Mark's Gospel is an abridgement, for did ever a book begin so?

Within this prelude can be recognized two paragraphs which come easily away as self-contained units, the story of the baptism of Jesus, introduced by "it came to pass" (so R.V.), and that of his temptation, introduced by one of Mark's favourite expressions of introduction "and immediately". They are of such a kind as to suggest (except on the somewhat clumsy and tasteless view that Jesus was in the habit of retailing his private religious experiences to others) that they had been formed in the tradition of the Church as a result of later reflection upon the person and work of Jesus as a whole, and as expressions of that faith in him as Son of God, and of that understanding of him, which had been arrived at through his resurrection and what had followed it. Here a great deal is being said, for these two stories provide a transcendental setting for the whole gospel story; but again there is extraordinary compression and considerable obscurity. We look in vain for historical or chronological details, or for any psychological basis. All is theological, that is, expressed in relation to the purpose of God.

At a moment unspecified, except as being "in those days", Jesus appears from a previously unmentioned Nazareth in Galilee, and after receiving baptism at John's hands perceives the heavens opened and the Spirit descending into him as a dove, and hears a voice from heaven addressing him in the words "You are my beloved [or only] Son [or, My Son the Beloved]; on you my choice rests". Jesus is thus to be understood as being from then on supernaturally endowed with the divine Spirit, but the symbolism of the dove continues to baffle the commentators, since nowhere in Judaism is there any clear association of a dove with the Spirit, and the least remote parallel is the representation in Egyptian and Persian cultures of the power of the king by a bird, sometimes a dove. The symbolism of the voice from heaven is fairly familiar in Judaism, and is plain, though what it here says is not. It appears to be a combination of Psalm 2.7, where God addresses the king as his son, whom on this day he had begotten, and to whom he promises the nations as his possession, and Isaiah 42.1, where God addresses Israel as his slave in whom he delights, and on whom he has put his spirit that he may bring forth judgement to the Gentiles. Jesus is thus divinely acknowledged as the divine son-king and as the slave of God, the true representative of Israel, who is the object of the divine choice. But it is not clear whether the present tense "you are" is a declaration to Jesus, who is previously ignorant of it, of an eternal status which is his, or, as Semitic idiom would allow, a decree adopting him into royal sonship from that time onwards. In either case the divine words are limited to a declaratory statement with no implications

13

expressed. No commission is given nor course of action indicated.

The scene changes from the Jordon river to the desert, and from baptism to temptation. All manner of reasons may be advanced for this juxtaposition, none of them wholly convincing, and it was perhaps Mark himself who first forged the connection with his extraordinary statement that the Spirit, on its reception, expels Jesus into the desert (the nature of the compulsion is not disclosed), with the implication that what had happened at the baptism had as its immediate and necessary consequence what was to happen in the desert. And what was that? Mark's story here must be taken on its own, and not glossed from, or read in the light of, the more extended accounts of Matthew and Luke. Their stories are of "the temptations", his of "the temptation". This is even more compressed and mysterious. It is content to say four things: the Spirit propels Jesus into the desert; he is there for forty days (a conventional biblical period of time) under temptation from Satan; he is with wild beasts; the angels minister to him. There is no mention of fasting. That the desert here stands for the abode of evil, the natural home of the demons and of Satan their Lord, is probable; that the mention of the beasts is meant to convey a picture of Jesus as the second Adam, improbable. Rather are the beasts the natural associates of evil powers (as in Psalm 91 and elsewhere in Jewish literature), and are set in contrast to the angels, whose ministry, unspecified, perhaps stands for the divine assistance in place of the Spirit, who here only compels Jesus. If the meaning of the whole is that the Son of God is victorious over Satan, this is not said, and a single sentence in which Jesus is spoken of not as the active assailant but only as the passive object of Satan's trial is hardly an effective way of saying it. Since no temptations are specified victory over them cannot be expressed.

These two stories are led up to by the first eight verses of the Gospel, which leave the impression of being not a self-contained unit of tradition, but a composition of the evangelist himself with the aid of tradition. They centre on John; not, however, upon him as an historical personage in his own right with a distinctive message and practice of his own, but on him in the single aspect of precursor. This is so with respect to either of his twin activities, that of the prophet-preacher of repentance, and that of baptism, in virtue of which he is here called not "the Baptist", which is a mere title, but "the baptizer". And John is himself made to say so in the only statement he is allowed to make in this gospel—the statement which immediately heralds the appearance of Jesus on the scene—that his water baptism is to be superseded by a baptism with holy spirit from one who is his successor and superior (though no indication is given of how John came by this knowledge) These twin activities, which require two different locations, the desert and the river, are somewhat awkwardly brought together by the condensed, and not wholly grammatical sentence "John the baptizer made his appearance in the desert preaching a baptism of repentance for the forgiveness of sins" (v. 4). The eschatological, or ultimate, character of these two activities is indicated both by the historically impossible statement that the whole of Judea and the total population of Jerusalem responded by coming to baptism, and also by the description of John's mode of dress and sustenance in the desert. This is intended not as sartorial or gastronomic information, but as theological. John is described in terms of Elijah, whose return to herald the messiah was current Jewish doctrine.

All this is taken back behind history to the divine will by the citation of Old Testament prophecies, combined and suitably adapted, of the divinely sent messenger-forerunner who is also the desert voice summoning to prepare the way of the Lord, who in this context becomes the Lord Jesus. This stands out in importance when it is observed that it is the only instance in the whole Gospel of the evangelist using the Old Testament in this proof-text manner. The link verses (14—15), in removing John from the scene and bringing Jesus on to it, bind them closer to each other. The ministry of Jesus, which is presumably supposed to follow immediately upon the baptism and temptation which

15

have prepared him for it, is not in fact dated with respect to them, or by any chronology, but solely by reference to John. But the translation "after John was arrested" (R.S.V., cf. N.E.B.) is probably too precise and historically-minded. The word used means "handed over" or "given up" (by God?), a neutral but also mysterious word; it is to be used later by Jesus of his own fate, which is thus here said also to be the fate of the precursor.

To all this—prophecy, prelude, and that to which it is a prelude—Mark attaches in his opening sentence the word *euaggelion,* gospel, "the beginning of the gospel of Jesus Christ", and to this word he returns in the link verses when he frames an epitome of the whole activity of Jesus with the words, "Jesus came into Galilee, preaching the gospel of God, and saying, 'The time is fulfilled, and the kingdom of God has drawn near; repent and believe in the gospel' ". This is a word which in its seventy-two occurrences in the New Testament is confined, apart from two instances in Acts and one each in I Peter and Revelation, to Pauline epistles, and to seven instances in Mark's Gospel and four in Matthew's, which are themselves taken from Mark's. It may thus have been a word of Pauline coinage, or have been taken by him from the terminology of the Christian mission field, to denote the message of salvation. The noun has no significant background in the Old Testament (though the corresponding verb has), but it was employed in the hellenistic vocabulary of salvation, especially in the cult of the divine saviour Emperor, though not with the precision it has in the New Testament, where it is used absolutely without qualifying genitive ("the gospel"), and always in the singular as the single gospel of the one God ("the gospel of God" cf. Rom. 1.1; 15.16; 2 Cor. 11.7; 1 Thess. 2.8f). Mark was probably responsible for introducing this word into the vocabulary of Jesus and of the gospel tradition. In doing so he attaches it so closely to the person of Jesus as to make it a synonym for him. Thus to lose one's life, or to leave one's family and possessions as a Christian, is to do so "for my sake and the gospel's sake" (8.35; 10.29; cf. 13.10; 14.9). This suggests that for Mark the scope of the word

16

extends right up to the time when he is writing, and so includes both what Jesus said and did, and also that preaching of which he is now the object in the Church, and through which he is being made present to men. "The beginning of the gospel of Jesus Christ" looks back to the point from which the present activity of the Church had its origin, and this is only partly a point in time, since in Old Testament prophecy and in the voice from heaven it issues from God in eternity. And Jesus in "preaching the gospel of God", and in calling for faith in the gospel and repentance in response to it, (though saying nothing of what this gospel is which is to be believed), is made to speak the language of the later Church.

This present activity of the Church thus provides Mark with the context for putting the units of tradition into serial form so as to make of them a single something, and from this context they are now to be understood; while vice versa the Pauline message of salvation now takes up these units of tradition into itself as its explication. But here there is something of a dilemma. If "gospel", like its companion word "preaching", denotes primarily for Paul the message proclaimed to the unbelievers, does this mean that Mark intends his work, which he calls not a book but a gospel, to be written message for unbelievers? If so, could he possibly have written in this highly compressed form, which takes so much for granted by readers already in the know? And would the units of tradition, which had been shaped for domestic use in the Church for the instruction of those in the know, have served this new purpose? If, on the other hand, Mark was writing for believers, was it to tell them what they did not know, in which case what was it that had made them Christians? Or was it to give them, whoever they were, in written form what in substance they knew very well already, in which case what was the reason for this transition from the spoken to the written word, and why is the result called a gospel?

If this is how the Gospel begins how does it end? So long as we are using the text of the A.V. there is no problem, except that here more than anywhere else there would be grounds for Augustine's verdict that the book is an abridgement. For after a vivid story of the visit of the women to the tomb, which ends with their flight from it in such terror that they say nothing to anyone about it, the narrative suddenly in 16.9—20 assumes the most summary form, and becomes little more than a list of appearances of the risen Lord to Mary Magdalene, to two disciples on a journey, to the eleven at a meal, concluded by a reference to his ascension. In all this the reader would look elsewhere in the Gospels of Luke and John for the originals of which this is a bare summary. But in the R.V. and all subsequent versions these verses are separated from what precedes by a large space. This reflects the verdict of all textual critics that these verses were not in fact written by Mark, but were added by a later hand to fill in a lacuna, and N.E.B. prints another attempt to do the same thing, and refers to the existence of others. Our earliest and most reliable manuscripts make Mark's gospel end with the words "And they went out, and fled from the tomb; for trembling and astonishment had come upon them; and they said nothing to anyone; for they were afraid" (16.8). But did a book ever end so? The answer to this question, once a knowledge of the textual evidence caused it to be asked, was emphatically "No". Mark must somehow have got over the stymie he seems to have laid himself by the silence of the women, and must have gone on, as the other evangelists went on, to describe appearances of the risen Lord. How else could a gospel end? And since the command of the young man at the tomb had been, "Go, tell his disciples and Peter, he goes before you into Galilee; there you shall see him, as he said unto you", (referring them back to a previous statement of Jesus himself (14.28), "All of you will be offended . . . but after I am raised up, I will go before you into Galilee"), Mark must have gone on to narrate an appearance of the risen Lord in Galilee. It is exceedingly awkward to come across a vacuum at this of all points in Mark's story, especially now that we know that Mark's is the first gospel. But we must suppose that something has happened; Mark's manuscript somehow, sometime, suffered damage, and we can only speculate how he continued beyond this point, and how he conceived his Gospel as ending. This is a natural view, and remains the view of many. But there are formidable difficulties in it. Since Matthew and Luke seem to leave Mark's Gospel at this point, it would seem that their copy of Mark ended in this way. Are we to suppose that there was only one copy of Mark abroad, and that a mutilated one? If it was mutilated, was there no one with enough wit in the church of its origin, or anywhere else, to supply the missing story which everyone knew?

So the possibility arises of interpreting the evidence differently. Perhaps the Gospel is not mutilated at all, and Mark deliberately laid down his pen at this point, as though to say, "the rest is silence". But then what? For what, now, is the direction and meaning of a narrative which reaches its goal in terrified silence, and what is the cause of the terror? What conception of the gospel dictates that its climax shall not lie in stories of the appearance of the risen Lord, but in an event which is only hinted at in the words "I will go before you into Galilee"? And since the Greek word rendered "go before", like its English equivalent, can mean either "go on in advance of" or "go at the head of" or 'lead", do we know for certain what is being said? Is the event which is being hinted at, and which causes such terror, a reunion of the risen Lord and the disciples who will find him already in Galilee when they get there, or is it that he will go at their head and lead them back to Galilee whence he had brought them? But if so, why and for what? And does the terror hint that something more is involved in resurrection than the return of Jesus from death—the beginning of the end of the world perhaps? It is very odd, is it not, if the gospel is a mutilated torso, and very mysterious if it is not?

In our search for the beginning Mark's Gospel thus disappoints. Both as a whole, and in its separate parts, it exhibits a high degree of theological interpretation, and we find ourselves here not at the source but already well downstream. This is highly offensive to our minds, since the tracking of origins is our special forte. St Paul declared the gospel to be an offence in his day to the Jews because they sought after signs, and to the Greeks because they were looking for wisdom. It is not our habit to seek after signs; but our type of wisdom is inseparable from a conviction that we can only understand something if we can track down its origin and trace its subsequent development from there. Whatever Mark's Gospel may be intended to supply, it is not this.

I conclude with a quotation from T. A. Burkill's study of the Gospel which significantly he entitles *Mysterious Revelation*:

> Although St Mark is concerned to delineate the earthly life of Jesus, his whole method of treating his subject is very different from what would normally be expected of a modern biographer. The gospel was composed for the edification of believers, not for the furtherance of the cause of historical research. The evangelist shows little or no interest in proximate causes, and he offers neither a history of the Master's upbringing nor a psychology of his inner feelings and reactions. Indeed the Jesus of St Mark's representation could owe nothing essential to his human ancestry and education, since what he is and what he does are simply the consequences of his divine origin and nature. It follows, therefore, that a right understanding of the gospel calls for a sustained effort on the part of the exegete to appreciate the evangelist's point of view, and to identify the questions which he is seeking to answer. (p. 4).

2

THE WORKS OF POWER

The understanding of any book involves of course an understanding of it as a whole and in its parts, and of its parts in relation to the whole. St Mark's Gospel provides a special case of this, if it be true that the materials available to him were for the most part self-contained traditional stories, each one as it were a miniature in its own frame, and that as an author he brought them all within a single frame in pursuit of a new conception of a single *euaggelion* or "gospel" in narrative form. Some of the most significant studies of Mark's Gospel in recent years, especially by English writers, have been concerned with the attempt to discover an overall pattern in it, and to investigate the parts as contributing to this pattern.

Dr P. Carrington in his work *The Primitive Christian Calendar* (1952) advanced the thesis, which he presented in a modified and elaborated form in his *According to Mark* (1960), that the Gospel is to be accounted for by Mark's intention of furnishing the Church at Rome with a continuous series of gospel lections for the liturgical year (the lections for each quarter exhibiting the same structural sequence and recurrent spiritual themes), and with two long lections, stretching from 10.46 to the end, for use at the Christian observance of the feasts of Tabernacles and Passover. This is a very precise and mathematically tight thesis, and allows little margin of error in dividing up the gospel correctly to get the right number of lections to cover the year. It has been criticized on the grounds

21

both that some of the lections so obtained appear to be too brief for their purpose, and also that the little knowledge we have does not point to such fixity of scripture reading in the Church at this time. John Bowman's *The Gospel of Mark* (1965) fastens on the Passover feast, and sees the model for the narrative character and arrangement of the Gospel in the Passover *haggadah,* that is, the long recital of the events of Israel's redemption which was part of the ritual of the Passover meal. Here the thesis is hardly tight enough. It is to be expected that echoes of the Exodus story will be found in a Christian writing, but for that story to have determined the character and sequence of Mark's narrative the parallels between that narrative and any possible *haggadah* form would have to be closer than appears here to be the case. This is not the defect of Dr A. M. Farrer's analysis in his *A Study in St Mark* (1951), modified subsequently in his *St Matthew and St Mark* (1954), where correspondences are so complex and subtle that it is not possible to do justice to them by a summary. He is the more particularly concerned with Mark's pattern, since he rejects the form-critical account of the origin of the materials as traditional units, and would ascribe not only the arrangement but the stories themselves to the evangelist's inspiration as a writer. The pattern he sees is a series of cycles which repeat themselves but also carry the story forwards, because each cycle prepares for, and prefigures the content of, the next, and each also prefigures the whole Christian message. One of the chief elements of the framework is a typological and numerical symbolism, according to which there are twelve healings of Israelites and one of a non-Israelite, pointing to the redemption of Israel and the mission to the Gentiles. Interwoven with this are the calling of twelve apostles in stages plus the call of Levi outside the apostolate, and the feeding of Israel and the Gentiles symbolized in the two feeding miracles by the numbers of the people fed, the numbers of the loaves, and the numbers of the baskets. Here the thesis is both mathematically and symbolically tight, and it is difficult not to suppose that if such a schematization was in the evangelist's mind he would have made it more immediately evident. Dr E. Best in his *The Temptation and the Passion* (1965) sees soteriology of two kinds as determining the shape of the Gospel, the binding of Satan, which the subsequent exorcisms show to have taken place already in the wilderness temptation, and the death for sin on the Cross which dominates the rest of the gospel. This depends, however, upon a particular and precise interpretation of the temptation story, where Mark is at his briefest and most non-committal.

There is very much which is highly illuminating in all these studies of Mark's pattern, more sometimes than in the commentaries which treat the contents of the Gospel piecemeal. None, however, can be said to have established its thesis and supplied us with all the necessary clues. It is therefore not surprising to find one of Mark's most recent commentators writing:

> The very fact that such widely differing principles of arrangement have been attributed to St Mark perhaps suggests that in searching the Gospel for a single and entirely coherent masterplan, corresponding to a set of clearly formulated practical purposes, scholars are looking for something that is not there, and attributing to the Evangelist a higher degree of self-conscious purpose than he in fact possessed.

He further quotes the judgement of the American scholar H. J. Cadbury that

> there is scarcely any thorough-going theological theory that permeates the whole narrative, and many things remain that a single unified theory would hardly have selected or left unexpurgated. The material was already miscellaneous, and St Mark tried as little to bring it into theological as into biographical articulation.[1]

With this justification we shall prescind from attempting to present an overall pattern, and shall be content with observations on the various kinds of material to be found in the Gospel.

Mark was provided with an end for his narrative in the death and resurrection of Jesus, although even here it takes a very curious turn. He was also supplied with a beginning, if there

[1] D. E. Nineham, *St Mark*, pp. 29f.

23

was a strong tradition of the association of the Baptist and Jesus. But as to what lay between there may have been little or no guide from tradition. It is difficult to say how far the plan of the Fourth Gospel is created by a theological purpose of presenting Jesus as the fulfilment of the spiritual themes of the Jewish feasts. If, however, there is genuine reminiscence behind its picture of Jesus as predominantly working in Jerusalem with occasional visits to Galilee, Mark's pattern (in which he is followed by Matthew and Luke) of a ministry in Galilee and its environs alone, culminating in a single visit to Jerusalem for death, may be his own conscious and deliberate creation. In view of the gospel's ending, with its hints of a return to Galilee—whatever the words are intended to mean—this choice of Galilee as the main scene, and of material which could belong to it, may have been determined less by geographical than by theological considerations. The unsophisticated but cosmopolitan and semi-hellenized Galilee is the scene of a divine revelation whose ultimate destination is the Gentiles, and Jerusalem, the home of Pharisaic and priestly orthodoxy, is the location of its opponents (3.22; 7.1) and the scene of its rejection. Within the Galilean story there is little by way of precise geography except movement around the sea of Galilee, Capernaum, and Bethsaida, while the movements outside Galilee and back again in 7.24ff baffle the commentators. Dr John Lowe was accustomed to describe them as resembling "the meanderings of an intoxicated fly". There are no dates; the events could have covered a few months or a number of years.

Quite apart from any supposed pattern in the gospel what immediately forces its attention upon the reader is what for want of a better word we call "miracle". This is so simply on the score of bulk. After the prelude (1. 1-15) four disciples are called, and the ministry then begins with an exorcism of a demoniac in the Capernaum synagogue (1. 21-8), followed immediately by the cure of Peter's mother-in-law of a fever (1. 29-31), and after sunset of many suffering from divers diseases, and by many exorcisms (1. 32-4). The next morning Jesus announces to the disciples that he must go elsewhere to the surrounding small towns to proclaim there as well, and this proclaiming is said to be accompanied throughout Galilee by exorcism (1. 35-9). The story then continues with the healing of a leper, and on the return to Capernaum with the cure of a paralytic (1.40–2.12). After a series of disputations (2. 13-28) a man with a withered hand is healed in a synagogue (3. 1-6), and a vast crowd not only from Galilee, but from Judea, Jerusalem, Idumea, trans-Jordan, Tyre and Sidon, gathers at the report of what Jesus is doing, and he heals so many, so that the sick throng him to touch his garments, and he is surrounded by shouting demoniacs (3. 7-12). Jesus then creates the Twelve for the same double purpose of proclamation and exorcism (3. 13—19), and on returning to a house he is involved in controversy with Jerusalem scribes, who allege that he performs his exorcisms as one himself possessed and by the agency of the ruler of the demons (3. 20-30). After an incident concerned with his family (3. 31-5) chapter 4 is made up of parables until, on crossing the lake with disciples, Jesus stills a storm (4. 35-41). Immediately on disembarking he exorcizes a Gerasene demoniac (5. 1-20), and on recrossing the lake answers a call of Jairus, a ruler of a synagogue, to heal his daughter, and on the way to raise her from apparent death heals a woman of a haemorrhage which no doctors had been able to cure (5. 21-43). He then goes to his home town, which wonders at his reputed wisdom and his mighty works, and is there able to heal only a few sick because of their unbelief (6. 1-6). The Twelve are then sent out in pairs with power over unclean spirits, and they go out and preach repentance, exorcize many demons, and heal many sick by means of oil (6. 7-13). Herod hears of him and concludes from the report of his mighty works that Jesus is John the Baptist come back from the dead (6. 14-16), and this remark leads the evangelist to a flash-back on the death of the Baptist (6. 14-29). The Twelve return from their mission with reports of what they had performed and said, and Jesus retires with them to a desert place and feeds the five thousand (6. 30-44). Immediately the disciples cross the lake and in the storm Jesus walks to them on the water. (6. 45-52). On disembarking they are recognized, with the result that

> the people scoured that whole countryside and brought the sick on stretchers to any place where he was reported to be. Wherever he went, to farmsteads, villages, or towns, they laid out the sick in the market-places and begged him to let them simply touch the edge of his cloak; and all who touched him were cured (6. 55-6).

The first half of Chapter 7 is occupied with a dispute with Pharisees and Jerusalem scribes on the matter of clean and unclean (7. 1-23), but this is followed by a journey to the regions of Tyre, where Jesus is defeated in his plan to remain concealed, and from a distance he expels a demon from the daughter of a pagan woman (7. 24-30). On returning to the sea of Galilee via Sidon and the Decapolis he cures a man who is deaf and has a speech impediment (7. 31-7). Then follows the feeding of the four thousand (8. 1-10), the request by Pharisees for a sign, which is refused, and interrogation of the disciples on the two feedings when they complain that they have no bread in their boat (8. 11-21). On arrival at Bethsaida a blind man is cured (8. 22-6). From 8.27–9.13 there are Peter's confession of Jesus' messiahship and the instruction which follows it, and the Transfiguration and the conversation which ensues; but on rejoining his disciples Jesus performs the exorcism of a deaf and dumb boy which they had themselves been unable to do in his absence (9. 14-29). From 9.30 to the end of 10 brings Jesus through Galilee via Capernaum to Judea and the outskirts of Jerusalem, and is occupied throughout with teaching, except that the exclusive attitude of the disciples towards an exorcist using the name of Jesus in his work is rebuked (9.38-40), and on leaving Jericho Jesus restores the sight of a blind man named Bartimaeus (10. 46-52). At this point this kind of action ceases. In Jerusalem, perhaps significantly, there is but one miracle, and that the only destructive miracle attributed to Jesus, the withering of the fig tree by a curse.

Simply to rehearse in this way the sequence of events in the Markan narrative is to be reminded forcibly of the part played by "miracle" in it. This occupies some two hundred verses, or nearly one third of the whole Gospel, and nearly one half of it up to the point where Jerusalem is reached. In a religious document of the first century A.D. resting upon a Jewish background this is an extraordinary proportion. Extraordinary also is the way in which Mark chooses to initiate this sequence. After a summary statement linking the prelude with the ministry in Galilee, and an account of the call of four disciples, Mark brings Jesus to Capernaum for a continuous teaching ministry in the synagogue, and he notes that "they were astonished at his teaching; for he was teaching as one having authority and not as the scribes" (1.21f). The reader might well expect to be given at this point examples of this authoritative teaching which causes such astonishment, and Matthew has removed the whole statement to a context where he thought it naturally belonged, turning it into a comment on the sermon on the mount (Matt. 7.29). But in Mark no such teaching is given. What follows is a violent scene of conflict in the synagogue, in which a demoniac assaults Jesus and is expelled, and the astonished bystanders interpret the new teaching (with authority?) as being exorcism, and deduce from this single instance that Jesus is lord of the world of unclean spirits (1.27). From this beginning onwards the rapid succession of one story of this kind after another, generally told in rough but vivid style, as well as the summaries of Jesus' exorcistic and healing work and of its effects with which the evangelist chooses to punctuate his narrative, build up an overwhelming impression of the irresistible power of the wonder-worker or "thaumaturge". The precedent thus set by Mark has influenced Matthew and Luke, who take over most of this material from Mark, even if at times in an abbreviated and softened form, and who can even add similar stories of their own. But the resultant impression is not at all the same, for in their Gospels the miraculous does not constitute such a proportion of the whole, nor is it the driving force of the narrative in the same way. Thus in Matthew's Gospel seven of these stories are just strung together in a special miracle section after the sermon on the mount, while in Luke's long journey to Jerusalem (Luke 9.51–19.27), which gives his Gospel much of its distinctive character, there are only four of them. Clearly any estimate of Mark's Gospel must take into account the preponderance of this miraculous element in it. What conception of *euaggelion* was it which required this particular selection of material for its expression? Behind this question is another, which may not permit of an answer, namely whether Mark's conception thus expressed was a faithful reflection of how things had been, or a distorted picture of one who was not a thaumaturge by constant and deliberate intent, but only, as Renan held, *malgré lui*.

The form-critic is not able to be of much help here, since there is little by way of stereotyped form to indicate the part played by such stories in the Christian mission. It is true that generally the situation and complaint of the patient are first described in more or less detail, then the method of cure, also in greater or less detail, and finally the successful result; but unless for some strange reason it were to be told backwards an act of healing cannot be narrated otherwise. At times the account is brief, as in the healing of Peter's mother-in-law (surprisingly so for those who think that Peter's reminiscences lie behind Mark's Gospel), and in that of the man with the withered hand. At other times it is among the most prolix in the gospels, as with the exorcisms of the Gerasene demoniac and the epileptic boy. At times the patient is named, at times not. At times the cure is the main content of the story, as in the cases of the leper, the woman with a haemorrhage, the blind man at Bethsaida, and Jairus's daughter. At other times it is in the background, and what stands out as the sharp point in focus is some important pronouncement made in the course of it. This is so in the healing of the paralytic with its declaration that the Son of man has power on earth to forgive sins; in that of the man with the withered hand where the patient is little more than a cipher in a controversy over the sabbath; or in the case of the Syrophoenician's daughter with its telling dialogue from which emerges the principle "to the Jew first and then to the Greek" (cf. Rom. 1.16). In those cases where the miracle is less prominent the story can be more easily placed on the background of the teaching and practice of the churches. A formal and artificial element is the chorus ending, when the audience, either a crowd or disciples, show uncanny theological perception and utter the appropriate theological judgement which the reader is expected to share. Examples are: "A new teaching! With authority he commands the unclean spirits and they obey him" (1.27); or "Who then is this, that the wind and sea obey him?" (4.41); or "He has done all things well; he even makes the deaf hear and the dumb speak" (7.37). Yet there is no chorus at points where it might have been expected, to express astonishment at the magnitude of the miracle or at its deep theological import, e.g. in the feedings of the multitudes or the walking on the water. Dibelius may be right that the diffuse, detailed, and sensational character of some of these stories argues their origin in a hellenistic milieu with its love of story-telling, but there is no compelling reason against an origin in the folk culture of semi-hellenized Galilee. Those on the other hand which, like the feedings of the multitudes and the storm at sea, exhibit strong Old Testament colouring are more likely to have come under self-conscious literary influences. Thus the healing of the deaf-mute in 7. 31-37 would read more naturally as the healing of a deaf man only, for the operative word "*Ephphatha*", interpreted as "be opened", is directed to the ears, and the result is said to be that his ears were opened. Is then the additional operation on the man's tongue, with the result that he spoke plainly, dependent on the description of the man as a stammerer (in the Greek *mogilalos*) as well as deaf, and is this description itself imported from the single occurrence of this very rare Greek word in the Greek Old Testament version of Is. 35.5: "The ears of the deaf shall hear . . . and the tongue of the stammerers shall (speak) clear"?

More significant than the forms of the stories are their concepts and vocabulary, which lead into that strange twilight zone in the ancient world between medicine and magic which is appropriately described by the word "thaumaturgy", with its double connotation of marvel and effective action. In the nature of the case this will have left only few traces in literature, such as Philostratus's account of the first century A.D. itinerant ascetic teacher and thaumaturge Apollonius of Tyana. Since the uncovering in this century of so many Egyptian papyri emanating from the lower strata of society, such as, for example, the Paris Magical Papyrus, we are better informed about it. There are, of course, great differences here. In the gospels we are far removed from the farrago of recipes and spells, formulae and incantations, and the strings of outlandish words which occur in these writings, but there are also close similarities which are not to be minimized or ignored, for they give a precision to actions and words in the gospels which is concealed in the English versions. We are here in the world where, for example, healing is secured by touching the healer or his garments (Mark 3. 10; 5. 27-32; 6. 56); where resident healing power flows as a substance from one to another (Mark 5.30), and where healing potency is a commodity transferable to assistants (Mark 3.15; 6.7,13); where saliva is applied to tongue and eyes (Mark 7.33; 8.23), where the touch or grasp of the healer's hand, the supreme instrument of power, effects immediate cure (Mark 1.31,41; 5.41; 8.25); and we are also in the superstitious world of a Herod where reports of mighty works can bring fear that the Baptist has come back from the dead (Mark 6.14).

In his summaries Mark shows that he makes a distinction between healing and exorcism (Mark 1.34; 3.10f; 6.5,55f), and it may be deliberate that a wide variety of cures is selected for special description—restoration of sight, hearing, and speech, recovery from fever, from the defilement of leprosy and from bloody flux, from paralysis partial or total, and from apparent death—and that a vocabulary more varied than appears in the English versions is used to designate the sick. It is also noticeable,

30

however, that this distinction can be blurred, as when the ministry of both Jesus and of the disciples is summarized as preaching and casting out demons (Mark 3.14; 6.7; but cf. 6.13); and other acts of power tend to be assimilated to exorcism Not only those expressly called demoniac are treated as such. The epileptic boy is said to be possessed of a demon who refuses to speak, and the storm on the lake is addressed as a demon. This tendency can be seen continuing in Matthew, who calls the dumb man possessed (Matt. 9.32), and by Luke, the supposed physician, who turns the fever of Peter's mother-in-law into a demon (Luke 4.39). In these instances actions and language are employed which we know from other sources to have belonged to the techniques of thaumaturgy and exorcism. Thus in healing the deaf stammerer Jesus is found, like the thaumaturge, looking up to heaven and sighing (Mark 7.34). In the treatment of the leper he is both angry and—so the Greek word should probably be rendered—"roars at" him. He delivers the typical exorcistic "rebuke" to demons (1.25; 9.25), and the general statement, "he commands the unclean spirits and they obey him" (Mark 1.27) is exemplified in the case of the epileptic boy by the exorcistic formula, "Deaf and dumb spirit, I command you to come out of him and never enter him again" (Mark 9.25). The exorcisms are scenes of violent combat, in which knowledge of the opponent's name was believed to bring the mastery, so that the demons, anticipating assault, counter-attack with an anti-exorcistic oath naming Jesus. "What do you want with us, Jesus of Nazareth? You have come to destroy us. I know who you are, the Holy One of God", shouts the Capernaum demonic (1.24); and "What do you want with me, Jesus Son of the Most High God? I adjure you by God not to torment me" shouts the Gerasene, (5.7) who, on being compelled to yield his name, does so with the braggadocio that his name is Legion ("there is a whole regiment of us"). Both the Capernaum demoniac and the storm on the lake are reduced to silence by the word *phīmōthēti* which is found in magical papyri for a binding spell, and which may be rendered "be muzzled", and visible

31

evidence of the defeat and exit of the demon is provided by cries and convulsions, and in the case of the Gerasene by the destruction of the swine.

But it is not only the Galilean or Hellenistic underworld which is echoed in the Markan narrative. The following are significant extracts from jottings of an anthropologist friend after several years residence with an African tribe.

> In my area most miracle workers are diviners who possess, or are possessed by, a power of divination which enables them to sort out the root cause of many deaths, illnesses, mental disturbances.

> Witchcraft and sorcery are generally supposed to be the cause of all deaths, misfortunes, etc. It is particularly serious because it is hidden and destroys society from within, whereas theft and murder are open and public.

> Virtually all the more famous diviners are supposed to be possessed, and are pretty well bound at some time or other to be called mad.

> The argument in favour of them which is generally found most persuasive is that they cannot be bad men if they are cleansing the country from witchcraft. What reason could a bad man have for destroying evil?

> It is common when retailing stories of diviners and miracle workers to tell not one story of a miracle but several to make quite sure of convincing the listeners.

> It is generally recognized that miracle workers cannot function all day and everyday, and many withdraw at times.
> Most diviners and helpers have some servant associate-apprentices.

> Many diviners have a large clientele hanging around where they are performing, sometimes for days. Many of these come from far away and are short of food. The diviner must accept responsibility for them and may feed them from his own supplies and the offerings he receives. His concern about this is another sign that he is not using his power for selfish ends.

There is always a certain tension between diviners and miracle workers and the chiefs or the government. On the one hand the political authorities should want the country cleansed of witch-craft, jealousy, and sickness so that the community may flourish. On the other hand people with supernatural powers of healing may threaten the political authorities.

All great diviners and healers are recognized well outside their own tribal areas. Their deeds testify to their honest intent. The only way to discredit them is by showing that they do not cure as they are reputed to do. There is no question of discrediting them by showing that they are from the wrong group or are doing it for the wrong reason.[1]

Much of this echoes what one writer has called "the savage element" in the gospel, and it is an element not to be avoided; for if we are in search of beginnings it is perhaps here that we are most likely to find them—in the Jesus whom Rudolf Otto traced in the important fourth section of his *The Kingdom of God and the Son of Man* (1938) as having the distinctive features of a "charismatic" figure. If a delicate piety shrinks from this as sordid, and as appearing to place Jesus almost on the same level as the demoniacs with whom he deals, it may be pertinent to observe that there is other evidence in the gospels that he was not particularly fastidious about the company he kept.

But why does Mark record this great quantity of miracle, and how does he intend it to be understood in relation to the *euaggelion*? These are not easy questions to answer. Plainly for Mark it is an integral part of the Gospel and not an adjunct to it, but there is nowhere any explicit discussion or exposition of these actions in relation to the whole of which they are parts, as there is for example in the discourses in the Fourth Gospel. Since we cannot be sure how Mark envisaged the connection between the earthly ministry of Jesus and what it had led to, we cannot be sure whether he has recorded these actions as deeds of

[1] I am indebted to Dr Alison Redmayne for these extracts and for permission to quote them.

the past only, limited to Jesus or to Jesus and the Twelve, or as foundation events of the Christian mission, or whether he intended them as models continuous with the current faith and practice of the Church, and with those mighty works which were to be expected wherever the Christian mission went, for which Paul may be cited in support (Rom. 15.19; 1 Cor. 12.10,28; 2 Cor. 12.12; Gal. 3.5). The stories by themselves hardly provide answers to these questions, and they should not be given too easily a theological or spiritual interpretation. They are on the whole remarkably secular, and not at all obviously and immediately connected with religious faith. God is not mentioned in them except by demons. How then are they part of the gospel of God which Jesus is said to be proclaiming? They are not stories about God but about Jesus himself, and are so told as to show him as always and inevitably victorious, and to glorify him and his powers; but they give little indication of what he thought he was doing. For this reason they raise acutely questions of interpretation which they can hardly answer. Who is Jesus, and what is his relation to God? Only demons seem to know. Hints are thrown out in some of the stories, but seldom without some element of obscurity or artificiality. Thus the interpretative command to the leper to go and show himself to the priests and to make the requisite offering "as a witness to them" (1.44) is far from clear. Is it to be a witness of Jesus' power, or of his compliance with the law?—or should the phrase be rendered, as elsewhere, "as a witness against them", implying either unbelief on their part, or that the priesthood and its functions are soon to be overthrown? In the case of the paralytic the interpretation is very explicit in terms of the power of the Son of man on earth to forgive sins, but healing and interpretation are awkwardly joined, and are thought by some to belong to separate stories. Nor are we permitted in this or in other cases to proceed direct from the particular to the general, and to reach some overall interpretation that way; as, for example, that all sickness is due to sin and all healing some form of forgiveness. In the case of the man with the withered hand it is not clear how the issue which is stated starkly in the question, "Is it right on the sabbath to do good or evil, to save life or kill?" arises out of the situation in which a man not in danger of his life is simply present in the congregation; nor in the case of the epileptic whether the interpretative remark "this kind can come out only by prayer" implies a special category, and that otherwise prayer is not needed. And there is plainly an element of artificiality whenever the interpretation lies with the concluding chorus, whether of the crowd or of the disciples.

Mark may have gone some way in the direction of interpretation by his arrangement of the material and by the juxtapositions he has chosen to make. Thus the exorcism in the Capernaum synagogue, which is given a certain pride of place as the opening public event of the ministry, and which involves a conflict between holy spirit and unclean spirit, follows on the baptism and temptation where Jesus receives the holy spirit and is controlled by it. The leper is followed by the paralytic, perhaps as instances of the two concerns of religion on its cultic side, i.e., ritual uncleanness and sin. They lead in turn to a picture of Jesus associating with the unclean tax collectors and the sinners, and to his own summary of his mission in the double terms of a physician who is needed by the sick and not the healthy and of his summoning (inviting to the kingdom?) the sinners and not the righteous. The healing of the man with the withered hand is made to follow a previous conflict about the sabbath; and the lengthy description of the violent behaviour of the Gerasene (5. 3-5) matches in human nature the violence of the physical elements which has been stilled in the immediately previous story, with which a similar juxtaposition may be compared in Ps. 65.7, "He stills the roaring of the waves and the tumult of the peoples". It is plausibly suggested that the story of the blind man at Bethsaida in its form of a partial followed by a complete restoration of sight is intended to point forward to the next paragraph, where the partial understanding by men of who Jesus is is followed by Jesus' own revelation of himself to those who see more clearly. The placing of the restoration of Bartimaeus's sight immediately before the hailing of Jesus and of the kingdom of David at the triumphal entry into Jerusalem is surely intentional, for Bartimaeus is the only patient, apart from demoniacs, to make a christological confession of faith (significantly at this point in terms of the title "Son of David"), and on receiving sight is said to "follow Jesus in the way". The two feedings of multitudes, whatever their previous history in the tradition, are tied together by Mark through the curiously emphatic dialogue in 8. 14-20 where, in face of the disciples' incomprehension of a mysterious warning against the leaven of the Pharisees and of Herod and their concern over having only one loaf, Jesus interrogates them in detail about the numbers fed and the amounts left over at each of the two feedings; while the first feeding and the walking on the water which follows it are connected by the statement that the disciples' astonishment at the arrival of Jesus in the boat was due to their incomprehension of the miracle of the loaves (6.51f). In this way Mark can make one miracle lead into another, or into something non-miraculous which is nevertheless analogous with it. Behind this procedure there seems to lie a philosophy whereby physical events can have a more than physical connotation, and language can take on a certain ambivalence.

Thus there are two words which more than any other govern this kind of material in Mark's Gospel, namely *dunamis* or "power", (the plural of which, *dunameis* or "works of power" (Mark 6.2,14; 9.39), is very common in hellenistic writing, though not in the Old Testament, for supernatural acts of healing etc.), and its synonym, *exousia*, which has the added sense of authoritative power. Both are thoroughly physical, as when on being touched by the woman, Jesus is said to perceive an efflux of the *dunamis* resident in him (5.30), or when *exousia* over unclean spirits through exorcism is said to be transferred by him to disciples (6.7). Mark's use of these words, and the preponderance in his narrative of actions which exemplify them, serve to convey the strong impression of the *euaggelion* as one of extraordinary power in action. (It is this, rather than miracle

36

in the modern technical sense of the word, which denotes a contravention of the known laws of nature; the ancient world did not have such a hard and fast conception of nature and its laws). But what is the moral and spiritual content of this power and its relation to the gospel? In the case of *exousia* hints are thrown out by its connection in the Capernaum exorcism with the new teaching unlike that of the scribes, and in the healing of the paralytic with the authoritative power of the Son of man to forgive sins. *Dunamis* is not interpreted, but one cannot help being reminded of the strong association of the gospel with power in Paul, and in particular of his statement that the gospel is "the power of God unto salvation for everyone who believes" (Rom. 1.16). This is not necessarily to say that Mark is here dependent on Paul for his conception. Mark's dependence on Paul has often been debated, and has been as frequently denied as affirmed. Paul's statement here may not be peculiarly his own but a reproduction of a common Christian idea, and he is in any case concerned with something rather different, the gospel of justifying grace. It is, however, striking that two of the mighty works, the healings of the woman with an issue and of Bartimaeus, are interpreted by the statement *hē pistis sou sesōke se* (5.34; 10.52), in which the ambivalence of the two chief words *pistis* and *sesōke* permit either the physical sense "your confidence [i.e. in the thaumaturge] has made you well", or the theological and more Pauline sense "your faith [unspecified] has brought your salvation".

The relation to a gospel of salvation of the power and authority displayed in the exorcisms, to which other mighty works tend to be assimilated, is indicated on rather different grounds, though also somewhat enigmatically, in the exorcism in the Capernaum synagogue. It comes not from Jesus but from the demons and the audience. As a result of this single exorcism the audience enunciates a general truth that Jesus is master of the demon world, and this is a clue to all subsequent actions of this kind on the part of Jesus and of his disciples. This is not a necessary deduction, and would not presumably have been made whenever a thaumaturge or rabbi performed a successful exorcism. It depends on two hidden pieces of theology, both of which are given expression by the demoniac himself. The first is that evil spirits, as well as being individuals, constitute a totality or realm, whose destruction, according to a Jewish theology later than the Old Testament, portended the end of evil and was the prelude to salvation, and this corporate status is voiced by the demoniac on behalf of all when he says, "What do you want with us . . . you have come to destroy us" (1.24). The second is that Jesus is not simply another exorcist, but the one who is to effect the ultimate destruction of the whole demon world, which is alone able to penetrate his disguise and to address him as "the Holy One of God" (1.24; cf. 5.7—"Son of the Most High God").

The first of these two theological factors, that the fate of the whole kingdom of evil is involved in individual exorcisms, appears again in a passage which is of great importance as being the only passage of any length to treat of exorcism, but which is unfortunately obscure in both its language and its logic (Mark 3. 22-30). Jerusalem opponents account for the exorcisms, which are here presumed to have been already numerous, by the double hypothesis that Jesus is himself possessed ("he has Beelzeboul"), and that he exorcizes by the agency of the ruler of the demons, who may be the same person as Beelzeboul, or distinct from him and identical with Satan. Jesus' reply according to Mark is spoken "in parables", and it is difficult to discern what in it is statement of fact and what indirect parable. In the opening question, "How can Satan cast out Satan?", Satan is a corporate term for the whole kingdom of evil which is involved in individual exorcisms. Hence the continuation— "If a kingdom is divided against itself, that kingdom cannot stand; and if a house is divided against itself, that house will not be able to stand. And if Satan has risen against himself and has been divided, he is not able to stand but he is finished"—could in itself lead to the conclusion of the opponents: the end of Satan is indeed assured because there is already civil war in the kingdom of evil because Jesus is possessed. Dr Best, who wishes to take the words which follow—"no one can enter into the house of the strong man and plunder his goods unless he has first bound the strong man, and then he will plunder his house"—not as parable but as a factual statement that Jesus had once and for all bound Satan at the temptation (his successful exorcisms being the consequence of this) is forced to take the previous statement as "a half-humorous argument" in which Jesus "accepts the premise of the scribes that he has an evil spirit and shows that this leads to the conclusion that the downfall of Satan is assured; the premise must therefore be incorrect" (op. cit., p. 11). The irony however is not very evident, and the words are probably to be taken as a direct rebuttal in the form "If the kingdom of evil were at civil war it would be on the point of collapse, but this is not the case, and hence there is no civil war". The binding of the strong man will then be a genuine parable of what is involved in each successive exorcism.

The second of the theological factors, that Jesus is the destroyer of the kingdom of evil as being the Holy One of God (a designation used of him only in the synagogue exorcism) leads back into the prelude to the Gospel, to the voice from heaven at the baptism, to Jesus' reception of holy spirit there, to his expulsion into the desert by the same spirit, and to the preceding prophecy of the baptizer-forerunner which sets the scene for the whole ministry of Jesus—"there comes after me the mightier than I . . . I baptized you with water, but he will baptize you with holy spirit". Both the form and the interpretation of this prophecy appear to have varied in the early Church. Matthew and Luke agree here against Mark in having a contrast between a baptism of water and a baptism of holy spirit and fire, for which some conjecture an original "wind and fire", since *pneuma* ("spirit") in Greek without "holy" can mean wind, and what follows refers to the winnowing fan of separation and to the fire burning the chaff (Matt. 3.11f; Luke 3.16f). Luke probably saw the fulfilment of this prophecy in the wind and fire of Pentecost, when the Spirit which Christ receives from the Father at his exaltation is poured out on the disciples. He places a variant of the prophecy in the mouth of the risen Lord: "John baptized with water, but you shall be baptized in holy spirit not many days hence" (Acts 1.5), which plainly refers it to Pentecost. Its later recollection by Peter in this form links it to the Gentile Pentecost of Cornelius and his household (Acts 11.16). It does not follow that this is how Mark understood it. The association of the word "baptize" with the subsequent practice of Christian baptism, and the association of that baptism with the reception of the Spirit, have become so fixed in the mind by the Lucan picture as almost to exclude any other. It tends to conceal how remarkable an expression "baptize with holy spirit" is. The Greek word *baptizein,* apart from its technical use for baptism, means to dip, to plunge or immerse, and the element required is some form of liquid, generally water. In what sense, then, was the mightier one to plunge John's hearers in holy spirit? The spirit by which Jesus is invaded at his baptism and which drives him into the desert is not, indeed, represented as his possession, or as the sphere in which he operates, but as a compulsive agent. Nevertheless Mark represents him as being immediately engaged in conflict (on his first public appearance) with its opposite, described as "unclean spirit" (for which "unholy spirit" would be a not improper rendering), and this unclean spirit addresses him as "the Holy One of God". The events, even Jesus' reception of spirit, are physically or quasi-physically conceived, but what they denote is a supernatural conflict between God's holy one who is possessed by, and is the bearer of, holy spirit, and the victims of the demon realm possessed by unclean (unholy) spirit. The successful outcome of these conflicts is already the baptism of men in holy spirit. This is how even Luke appears to see it when he puts into Peter's mouth the summary, "You know the thing that happened over all Judea, beginning from Galilee after the baptism John preached, concerning Jesus from Nazareth, how that God anointed him with holy spirit and *dunamis,* who went about doing good to and healing all who were under the tyranny of the devil" (Acts 10.37f).

The designation "unclean spirit" occurs again regularly in Mark's gospel for the demons; the term "holy spirit", apart from a reference to David as inspired in uttering a psalm and to the promise of the Spirit's aid to the disciples when on trial (12.36; 13.11), occurs only once, in the dialogue about Beelzeboul (3.29). If it is Mark's intention to say that the whole healing ministry of Jesus is already his plunging men in holy spirit, then what has generally been regarded as the most terrible statement in the Gospel (that all human slanders are pardonable, but that "whoever slanders the Holy Spirit can never be forgiven; he is guilty of an eternal sin") becomes more intelligible. For the proposition that the holy one of God, who is baptizing men in holy spirit, acts as he does because possessed by unholy spirit and through the agency of the ruler of the kingdom of evil, perverts the ministry of Jesus at its very heart, and renders the gospel at one of its most factual and physical points completely unintelligible. That Mark as a Christian believed in the Christian's present possession of the Holy Spirit through faith in the Risen Lord and through baptism in his name is probable enough. How he envisaged the relation between this possession of the Spirit and Jesus' baptism of men in holy spirit in his earthly ministry he does not tell us. This is part of the wider question of how he envisaged the relation of the past events he was narrating to the *euaggelion* of his own day which he wrote to serve.

3

THE TEACHING

It is a peculiarity of Mark's Gospel that to a greater extent than the other gospels, and perhaps than any other writing, it is a unity made up of units. The units are there for all to see. The unity may continue to escape detection since it is clearly not that of a systematic writer, but unless positively disproved it must be presumed to be that of a single *euaggelion* moving from a predetermined beginning to a climax which is also a fresh beginning, with a strong impression being built up on the way. This impression is predominantly that of an incessantly active Jesus. The gospel of Jesus Christ, which is also said to be the gospel of God proclaimed by him in the near approach of God's rule, begins with an exorcism, and continues with a series of similar actions which provide the main driving force of the narrative, and which serve to characterize the gospel as one of manifested power. In so far as this power is interpreted it is in the mythological terms of the destruction of the rule and realm of Satan. This impression is maintained by Luke, not so much in his Gospel as through such speeches in Acts as make any reference at all to the earthly ministry of Jesus, whether these are to be seen as reports of what was actually said or reflections by Luke upon the ministry which he has already recorded. So at Pentecost Peter presents Jesus as "a man attested to you by God with mighty works and wonders and signs which God did through him in your midst as ye yourselves know (Acts 2.22), and to Cornelius he particularizes the word of God to Israel and the peace gospelled by Jesus Christ, the Lord of all, as "the word which was proclaimed throughout all Judea, beginning from Galilee after the baptism which John preached, how God anointed Jesus of Nazareth with the Holy Spirit and with power, how he went about doing good to and healing all who were oppressed by the devil; for God was with him" (Acts 10. 36-38), while he proclaims that it was by virtue of the name of Jesus that the lame man at the Temple gate had been healed, in which name alone was salvation (Acts 4. 10-12). Even when reference is made to Jesus' teaching it is as to a "prophet mighty in deed and word"—in that order (Luke 24.19).

There are two curious elements in Mark's narrative, however, which may point to a concern to characterize not only what the gospel had been in its beginnings but what it still had to be. The first is that, although it is power rather than compassion which prompts the mighty works (compassion is mentioned only in connection with the two feedings, in the first compassion for the crowd as a shepherdless flock and in the second for their hunger after a three day's sojourn), they were on any showing acts of beneficence, yet they are met with bitter hostility from opponents, generally specified as scribes or Pharisees (2.6; 3.2,22; 8.11; 9.14). Further, since these are in conflict with Jesus and Jesus is in conflict with Satan it is implied that they are on the devil's side. Such perversity is nowhere adequately explained, and it plays no part in the ultimate arrest of Jesus and in the charges against him at his trial. It may thus be a reflection back into the earthly actions of Jesus of a later hostility between Judaism and the Church which had originally arisen on other grounds.

The second is the puzzling element of secrecy which is introduced into certain miracle stories. The demons are habitually forbidden to speak because they know who Jesus is (1.34; 3.12), the leper is strictly charged not to publish his cure (1. 43f); those who witness the raising of the daughter of Jairus are told to keep it quiet (5.43); while in the case of the deaf-stammerer, who is taken away on his own to be healed, the crowd is ordered to tell no one about it but disobeys the order (7. 36-7), and the blind man at Bethsaida is not allowed to enter the village (8.26). It may be that these stereotyped injunctions should not be taken, as by Wrede and others, to constitute—along with similar injunctions to silence over the person of Jesus (8.30; 9.9) and an esoteric element to be found at times in his teaching—a single over-all doctrine of messianic secrecy imposed by the evangelist upon the gospel story. It may be rather that each instance should be taken on its own and examined separately for a possible cause relative to it, if only for the reason that any such doctrine is not applied consistently. Thus both individual and mass healings are recorded as performed without compunction in circumstances of the utmost publicity, and so as to evoke the widest acknowledgement. The Gerasene is even commanded to publicize his cure and to become a missionary thereby (5.19f). Even so it is impossible to eliminate all artificiality from these injunctions, especially when attached to mighty works, both because in some instances (e.g. in the case of Jairus's daughter) what was enjoyed could not possibly have been carried out, and also because they conflict with the essential nature of the acts to which they are attached. It is of the essence of mighty works that power shall be manifested, and that they shall not only be done but shall be seen to have been done. They cannot, except on paper, both be designedly done and in the event wished undone. It may be that Mark was here contriving, though not with any consistency, to bring actions which in themselves bespoke success, and which proclaimed the power of Jesus and of God through him, into the larger and contemporary context of a gospel which had become a gospel of power only through the resurrection of the powerless, rejected, and crucified Christ.

The apostolic preaching as represented in Acts and Paul does not contain any reference to the teaching of Jesus, and "Teacher" was not a title under which the crucified and exalted Lord was proclaimed. The nearest approach to it is the application to him of the Deuteronomic promise, "the Lord God will raise up for you a prophet from your brethren as he raised me up. You shall listen to him in whatever he tells you. And it shall be that every soul that does not listen to that prophet shall be destroyed from the people" (Acts 3.22f; 7.37). Nevertheless the gospels are themselves evidence that the tradition which saw him as a thaumaturge and handed on his mighty works saw him also as a teacher and handed on his teaching, and so preserved it in solution. Sometimes these two elements are found together, as in the double question of his fellow-townsmen, about Jesus, "Where did this man get all this? What is this wisdom given to him, and such mighty works wrought by his hands?" (6.2); or in Mark's editorial comment that the apostles returned from their mission of proclamation and healing and reported "all things, all they had done and all they had taught"—again in that order (6.30). One of the problems which the tradition posed to the evangelists as its redactors was how these two elements, which may have reached them separately and along different lines, were to be combined and orchestrated within a single composition. Was Jesus a rabbi who happened also, like other rabbis, to heal and exorcize, or was he a thaumaturge who took upon himself also to teach, or was he neither, who yet did both? Each evangelist has his own proportions in dealing with this problem. In Mark's Gospel it is a question of the place and function of the teaching in a story dominated by the mighty works, and of its relation to the continuing gospel of Mark's own day.

The situation is somewhat paradoxical in that while, both absolutely and proportionately to its size, his Gospel contains far less of the teaching of Jesus, there is, both absolutely and proportionately to the other gospels, far more reference in it to the activity of Jesus as a teacher. This may be seen from an examination of Mark's vocabulary in the matter. Thus the word *kērussein,* to proclaim, is found more often in Mark's Gospel than in any other New Testament book. A word taken from the missionary vocabulary of the Church, it can cover the preaching of the post-Resurrection Christian message (13.10; 14.9), the divine mission of the Baptist (1.4,7), the initial proclamation of

Jesus as a divine mission (1.14,38f), the initial proclamation of the twelve as missionaries (3.14; 6.12), and the publicizing by others of the healing acts of Jesus (1.45; 5.20; 7.36). The word *euaggelion,* gospel, which can go with it, is, as has already been noted, a distinctive word of Mark's gospel. It is used eight times, generally in close association with the person of Jesus, whereas Matthew reproduces only four of these instances, and Luke and John do not have the word at all. *Didaskein,* to teach, is also found more often in Mark's Gospel than in any other New Testament book (Mark—17, Matthew—14, Luke—16, John—8, Acts—16, Pauline epistles—13—remarkable figures considering the comparative brevity of Mark's Gospel), and is used as an inclusive term for the activity of Jesus in synagogue or temple (1.21; 6.2; 11.17; 12.35; 14.49), for his instruction of crowds in either a resident or an itinerant ministry (2.13, 4.1f; 6.34; 10.1) and of disciples, and of their instruction of others (8.31; 9.31; 6.30). More than once it is in the imperfect tense to denote a customary activity, and at 10.1 Jesus is said to teach the crowd "as his custom was". The corresponding noun *didachē,* teaching, which is also more frequent than in any other New Testament book, is used of his teaching in synagogue or temple and of the crowds (2.22,27; 4.2; 11.18; 12.38). Further Mark uses an expression not found in the other gospels, "He used to speak to them the word" (2.2; 4.33; 8.32), which also smacks of the later missionary vocabulary of the Church.

In the Gospel Jesus is addressed as "Rabbi" three times, twice by Peter and once by Judas, and by Bartimaeus with the stronger "Rabbouni"; while in Matthew's gospel this address is used twice by Judas, and in Luke's not at all. Only John has it more frequently than Mark. Its chief Greek equivalent, *didaskalos,* (cf. John 1.38; 20.16; Matt. 23.8) is used in address to Jesus more often by Mark than by Matthew, but slightly less often than by Luke. Though not a title in the later sense of referring to "Rabbi So-and-So", it was a mode of address to the learned which was deeply reverential as well as functional. Coming from a root which meant "master" in contrast to "slave", its equivalent is "magister" or "master", one who teaches the divine truth as it is contained in the Law (which is the specific sense of "to teach" in the Old Testament and rabbinic writings), and who is in a position of authority over his devotees. Hence Luke, who avoids the word rabbi, reserves *didaskalos*, teacher, for those occasions when Jesus is questioned as a teacher by Pharisees (with one exception), and (also with one exception) uses the Greek word for "master" (*epistatēs*) for those occasions when he is addressed by his disciples as their personal lord. Thus Jesus is depicted not as one who happened to open his mouth from time to time, but as one of the scribes; though how far he underwent scribal training and received authorization is disputed. The necessary correlative of rabbi or *didaskalos* is *mathētai*, disciples, a technical term for the adherents or pupils of a rabbi. Apart from its use in Acts absolutely (the disciples) as a general term for Christians, it is not found in the New Testament outside the gospels, since in the epistles Jesus was no longer being thought of as a rabbi. In Mark's Gospel the disciples, as the pupil-companions of Jesus and as the recipients of his instruction, figure more largely than in Luke's, and as largely (if comparative length is taken into consideration) as in Matthew's and John's.

Thus a study of Mark's vocabulary shows him going out of his way to sketch in outline the lineaments of a Palestinian rabbi. What is puzzling is that the sketch is not really filled out like that of the thaumaturge, and what for want of a better word we call the "teaching" of Jesus is limited in scope, and occupies a subordinate place in a narrative of mighty works. Mark may underline the activity of Jesus as preacher and teacher, but it is difficult to discover from his Gospel what exactly the preaching and teaching can have been. Thus Jesus is said (1.14-15) to proclaim in Galilee the gospel of God and to summon men to "believe in" the gospel (a use of "believe" without parallel in the New Testament), which gospel is later coupled with himself as that for which men are to be ready to forsake all possessions and to lay down their lives. But what this gospel is is not specified, except that it involves the near approach of the rule of God. He is then said to teach in synagogues with such authority as to be distinguished from the scribes, but no specimen is given of this teaching, and it is exemplified rather by exorcism. He is said to speak the word to the crowds (2.2), but no content is given to this word, and what follows is the healing of the paralytic. Again when an enormous mixed crowd gathers from all quarters of Palestine (3.7ff) he is said to speak the word to them in many parables as they were able to hear, and not to speak to them apart from parables, but all that is given is the somewhat meagre collection of parables in 4.1-23, which are in any case to be made intelligible only to disciples. Similarly when the Twelve are sent out on mission they are given elaborate instructions as to their behaviour, but nothing is said of their message, except that it is a preaching of repentance; and when they report back what they had done and said the reader knows that the former means exorcism and healing, but he has no inkling of what the latter might have been. Both the gospel and the teaching of Jesus seem to be assumed. What then is the teaching which is recorded, and what purpose is it intended to serve in relation to the whole book and to the gospel in Mark's own day?

Leaving aside the discourse of chapter 13, which requires special treatment as belonging closely with the passion narrative, the teaching may be said to fall roughly into five sections. Section A (2.1–3.6) consists of three debates, the first with Pharisaic scribes over the propriety of eating with sinners, which is attached to the call of Levi, and issues in the pronouncement "I came not to summon [to the kingdom?] the righteous but sinners"; the second with persons unnamed over the fact that, while the disciples of John and of the Pharisees fast, the disciples of Jesus do not, and leading to a statement that fasting is inappropriate at wedding time (to which are attached parabolic sayings on the incompatibility of what is new with what is old); and the third with Pharisees over the contravention of the sabbath by Jesus' disciples, leading to the judgement that the sabbath was made for men, and that the Son of man is Lord of it. These three debates are bracketed between two miracle stories in which the weight falls upon the accompanying controversy rather than on the healing itself. At one end is the healing of the paralytic through the power of the Son of man on earth to forgive *sins*, which links it to the following story of eating with *sinners*. At the other end is the healing of the man with the withered hand on the sabbath, which is linked with the immediately preceding sabbath dispute, and in which it is not others but Jesus who takes the initiative as lord of the sabbath, and who makes it a test case of what is and what is not permissible on the sabbath. The section is rounded off by reference to a curious coalition of Pharisees and those called Herodians, who are not easy to identify, and who may belong to the pro-Pharisaic Herod Agrippa I of Mark's day rather than to the Herod Antipas of Jesus' day. They plot Jesus' death, which is a surprising turn of events, since the disputed actions hardly warrant the death penalty, and no mention is made of them when eventually Jesus is brought to trial.

Sections D runs from 9.33 to 10.31, and consists of five units, picture of the contrast between the physical family of Jesus who are standing outside and those around him who are said to be his true family (3. 31-5), and it consists of a discourse on a single subject, the parabolic teaching of Jesus, of which it provides a rationale. This is done by means of the parable of the sower, told to the crowd, and its private interpretation, as the key to all the parables, which is told to an uncomprehending inner circle of those around Jesus. In between comes the statement that God has already given the mystery of the kingdom to the inner circle in contrast to those outside, to whom all things happen in parables so as to prevent their understanding, repentance, and forgiveness. To this are added three parables of a similar kind, that of the lamp which is not to be put under a bed but on a lampstand, together with sayings on the need to hear and be receptive, that of the seed growing of itself, and that of the mustard seed. The section is rounded off by a general description of Jesus' parabolic method—he never taught the crowd except by parables, and he always followed it with a private interpretation to the disciples

Section C (7. 1-23) resembles A in that the setting is a bitter conflict between Jesus and Pharisees and Jerusalem scribes over conduct of some of Jesus' disciples which contravenes Jewish religious practice. It resembles B in being a discourse on a single subject, clean and unclean, built up out of diverse materials, and in providing a particular instance of Jesus interpreting a public utterance to his disciples in private. It begins from a complaint at the established behaviour of certain disciples in eating with defiled, that is unwashed hands, and in this way contravening not only Pharisaic but Jewish practice in general. This practice is said to be based upon the scribal interpretation of the Old Testament called "the tradition of the elders", and in the reply this is condemned from the Old Testament as being human tradition, whose observance involves neglect of God's commandment. This is exemplified by reference to the commandment to honour parents and its evasion by Korban, and this in turn leads into instruction of a crowd, especially summoned for the purpose, to the effect that defilement can arise only from what is internal in man and not from what is external to him, which statement is said to be a parable, and is privately elucidated to uncomprehending disciples.

Sections D runs from 9. 33 to 10. 31, and consists of five units mostly concerned with aspects of discipleship. In the first (9. 33-7) the truth that among disciples the first is to be last is illustrated from the child to be received "in my name". The second (9. 38-50) is a series of separate sayings spliced together to form an articulated catechetical unity by *step-parallelism*, that is, by the use of interlocking words and phrases. Thus "in my name" and "child" are picked up in the statements that no one can do a mighty work or give a cup of water "in my name" without being on Jesus' side or gaining a reward, and that whoever offends a "little one" had better be "cast" into the sea. "Offend" and "cast" are then picked up in the injunctions to be rid of the "offending" hand, foot, or eye rather than to be "cast" into Gehenna or the "fire"; and "fire" is then picked up in the statement that everyone is salted with fire. The third (10. 1-12) is a reply to a test question put by Pharisees on divorce, in which appeal is made behind the Deuteronomic law to God's ordinance in creation to establish the indissolubility of marriage, which is then privately interpreted to disciples in terms of a Church rule. The fourth (10. 13-16) shows Jesus in conflict with disciples over their treatment of children on the grounds that the kingdom of God belongs to such, and must be received as such. In the fifth (10. 17-31) the demand is made of the rich man who had kept all the commandments from his youth that he does the one thing necessary for eternal life, namely, to abandon all his possessions and become a disciple. This leads out into instruction of the disciples on the virtual impossibility, apart from an act of God, of the rich entering the kingdom, and to a promise to those who have left all for Jesus and the gospel of new families and possessions along with persecutions in this age, and of eternal life in the coming age.

Section E runs from 11.27 to 12.44 and is the only one to be located in Jerusalem. It consists basically of five debates, to which a parable has been added. It begins with a challenge from a new group of opponents—high priests, scribes and elders—on the source of Jesus' authority, which is met by a counter-question on the source of John's baptism, and refusal to answer the counter-question brings refusal to answer the original question. This is followed by a parable which is so plainly allegorical that the opponents cannot fail to see that they themselves are the labourers in the vineyard who maltreat and kill the messengers and finally the beloved son. There follows a test question from Pharisees and Herodians about the payment of tribute money, which leads through a counter-question to the pronouncement, "Render to Caesar what is Caesar's, and to God what is God's". The Sadducees then pose a conundrum designed to prove their doctrinal position that resurrection is unscriptural and impossible, and are pronounced to be in great error for their ignorance both of the power of God to transform material into spiritual life and of the scriptures. Then in reply to the request of a single scribe for a judgement on the debated question of the prior commandment Jesus combines the commandments of the love of God and the love of the neighbour; and when the scribe comments that this is greater than all sacrifices he is told that he is not far from the kingdom of God. Finally Jesus himself takes the initiative and queries the adequacy of the scribal title "Son of David" for the messiah by appeal to Ps. 110.1, where David himself addresses the messiah as "Lord". The section is rounded off by an excerpt of teaching in which the scribes are condemned as a class for ostentation, pretence, and greed in eating up widows' houses, and a poor widow is commended for giving of her poverty in the temple.

This last section has certain resemblances to A, since it also consists basically of five debates, all initiated by Jewish officials except the last in which Jesus takes the initiative, and in it the strange coalition of Pharisees and Herodians recurs. These two sections have for this reason attracted special study, and the suggestions have been made either that the first came to Mark as a written source and provided a model for his creation of the second, or that originally they belonged together, and came to Mark as a single unit of conflict stories which Mark split into two, advancing the plot of the Pharisees and Herodians to the period of the Galilean ministry, because it was in fact a different coalition in Jerusalem which had secured Jesus' death. There are however differences. Whereas in the earlier it is because Jesus is involved in the behaviour of his disciples that he is challenged, in the later the disciples play no part. Significantly in Jerusalem and in the context of the passion he is attacked alone. Further, in introducing the parable of the wicked husbandmen with the words "he began to speak to them in parables" and the condemnation of the scribes with the words "and in his teaching he said", Mark approximates this section to B, which is introduced with "And he taught them many things in parables, and in his teaching he said. . . ." (4.2).

53

What is involved in this particular selection of teaching by Mark? For while the view that Mark has here arranged all the teaching he was aware of cannot be disproved, it is, in the light of the evidence of the other gospels and of indications elsewhere in the New Testament of a strong catechetical interest, highly unlikely. Mark has presumably chosen to reproduce from a wider stock that particular teaching which served his purpose in writing. The form-critic will point out what a high proportion of it is set in the context of controversy. To a considerable extent the teaching of Jesus in Mark's Gospel means not a sequence, and still less a system, but a succession of single authoritative sentences, each bringing to an end a dispute over some issue raised by opponents with hostile intent. Matthew and Luke add very little of this kind, and hence do not produce the same impression. For them, as for the later author of the Gospel of Thomas, Jesus the teacher means one who delivers discourses composed of sequences of sayings or parables. This is at a minimum in Mark's gospel. The controversial form is well attested, particularly in Jewish sources, and it establishes the teaching of Jesus as rabbinic, at least in style.

In an essay entitled "Jesus as Teacher and Prophet" [1] Dr C. H. Dodd analysed the rabbinic and the prophetic features in the gospel picture of Jesus, and he enumerated the prophetic features as follows:

(a) the impression given that Jesus is a spirit-possessed person; (b) the authoritative "Amen, I say to you", and the elevated, rhythmic character of his teaching; (c) the utterance of predictions and the performance of symbolic acts; (d) the conviction of a vocation from God which is directed to the destiny of the nation; and (e) the ethical emphasis of his teaching, with its demands for righteousness above ceremonial and for repentance. It is evident how much of this impression is derived from the contents of the other gospels and how little of it from Mark's, where spirit-possession is a matter of mighty works, and

[1] *In Mysterium Christi*, ed. G. K. Bell and A. Deissmann (1930).

elevated or rhythmic sequences are very few, where there is reticence about Jesus' vocation, where it is indiscriminate crowds rather than the nation which is addressed, and where the kingdom is not expounded in terms of righteousness but left largely unexplained. The same results would be arrived at if the starting point were R. Bultmann's three categories for the teaching of Jesus: logia or wisdom sayings, prophetic and apocalyptic utterances, and declarations related to the Law and to community discipline. Paradoxically it is the rabbinic rather than the prophetic form through which Mark conveys the authority of Jesus, an authority which is nevertheless of such a kind that it has also to be stated to be non-rabbinic (1.22). J. M. Robinson probably goes too far in a search for unity and over-theologizes when in his study, *The Problem of History in Mark* (Chapter IV) he synthesizes the miracles and the debates, the actions and the words, as two aspects of the same thing, the eschatological attack upon, and resistance to, Satan. The "tempting" of Jesus by the Pharisees when they pose test questions on divorce or tribute (10.2; 12.15) is not necessarily to be regarded as on the same level as the temptation of Satanic opposition, while on the whole the teaching is not presented as that which brings about the rule of God, but rather as commenting upon or defending positions already achieved. Nevertheless it is the case that such a series of controversies, so stripped down as to show Jesus always and inevitably emerging as victor with the last word, was more congruous than any other type of teaching with Mark's story, which is primarily one of power through mighty works.

Two further features tally with this rabbinic form, although not without a certain artificiality. The first is an appeal to the Old Testament text typical of rabbinic debate. In most cases, however, this does not seem to belong to the heart of the matter, but to be attached somewhat loosely as a secondary element. Thus, in the debate on sabbath observance, the freedom of the disciples is primarily determined by appeal to the principle that the sabbath was made for man, and to the right of the Son of man to determine what is or is not permissible in relation to it, and it is not clear how the behaviour of David with his companions when hungry (but not on a sabbath) justifies the action not of Jesus but only of his disciples on a sabbath (when not said to be hungry). Similarly the Sadducees' attempted disproof of resurrection by a *reductio ad absurdum* is answered by an assertion of the power of God to transform an earthly into a heavenly existence, and the further proof of resurrection by a text from scripture reads like an addendum. The citation from Isaiah in 7. 6-7 serves to generalize a specific charge against a particular tradition of the elders as leading to neglect of a particular commandment; and that in 4.12 simply grounds in scripture the inability to understand the parables. In the discussion of divorce the authority of Deuteronomy is abrogated by appeal to the original will of the Creator with words which are not expressly stated to be a quotation from Genesis. Only in the summary of the commandments and in the question about the Son of David does the scriptural text belong to the heart of the argument, in the first case to establish the essence of Judaism, and in the other to undermine one form of its messianic hope (12.29f, 36). It is possible, therefore, that the appeal to scripture in these debates belongs to a later stage, when the Church was looking for scriptural justification for Christian positions already established on other grounds.

The second feature is the part played by the disciples. This is a technical term for the personal pupils of a rabbi, who sit at his feet, receive his instruction, and are under his authority. From the opening act of the ministry in Galilee, when the first four are, without preparation or explanation, summoned and leave all to follow him, until the point in Jerusalem where all desert him, Jesus hardly ever appears in Mark's Gospel without them. Along with "disciple" goes the word "follow", which is to be taken literally as meaning "to go along with" in the physical as well as any other sense (1.18; 2.14; 6.1; 8.34; 9.38; 10.21, 52). The disciples share their teacher-master's movements, career, and destiny, and are involved in his actions and attitudes, as he is in theirs. Thus it is they who are challenged because he eats with sinners (2.16), as it is he who is implicated when they have adopted a mode of life which results in not fasting, in disregard of sabbath regulations, and in eating with unwashed hands (2.18; 2.23f; 7.5). But in Mark's Gospel this picture has quite lost perspective, for when the word "disciple" is introduced for the first time into the narrative on the occasion of the meal with the publicans and sinners Jesus is said without explanation to be already surrounded with a very large number committed to his cause and attitude (2.15). In 3.7 this is increased to a vast horde (*plēthos;* cf. 5.24 *ochlos*, "crowd") from Galilee which is now said to be following, and in 3. 32-4 those to whom he points as his true family are said to be the multitude sitting around him (the word is *ochlos*, generally used for the vast audience addressed by him). It is these same people, those around him (his entourage), who with the Twelve are given the explanation of the parable of the sower, so that when it is said (4. 34-5) that he never spoke to them apart from parables and that he interpreted in private to his own disciples, any distinction between an inner group, a larger entourage, and the multitude, has become blurred. This picture of Jesus permanently accompanied by a vast train of personal adherents, who have presumably left family and possessions to follow him, is scarcely feasible. The Palestinian rabbi has here taken on the features of a leader of a mass missionary movement, and the reason the picture is out of focus is that it has become a paradigm of the Lord and his Church in Mark's own day.

This indication in Mark's record that he is less concerned with original meaning and historical verisimilitude than with the import of the teaching for the contemporary Church may be illustrated from the discourses in Chapter 4 and Chapter 7. Chapter 4, in which Mark gives his only collection of parables, is fairly evidently the composition of the evangelist, and is often the despair of the commentator. It is made up of four parables—the sower, the lamp, the seed growing of itself, and the mustard seed—of which the common point may originally have been that the rule of God takes the paradoxical form of something

57

5

seemingly improvident, hidden, unrecognized, and small, which will yet produce the desired result. Into these Mark inserts as explanation a saying, "To you (presumably disciples) God has given the secret of the kingdom of God, but to those outside (those who are not disciples) whatever happens, happens 'in parables', with the result that they do not understand, do not repent, and are not forgiven" It is probable that this saying, outside its present context, was intended as a comment on the ministry of Jesus as a whole—to those not in the know all that is going on is "in parables", i.e. is enigmatic—and that Mark has taken it to refer to parables, and through its use here imparts to the teaching of Jesus an esoteric quality which necessitates private elucidation to an inner circle. This is as artificial as the secrecy attached to the miracles, for as it is the essence of mighty works to be seen to have been done it is of the essence of a parable that it should be readily intelligible. What, however, makes parabolic speech a hazardous and often inefficient form of communication is that, unless it is of a generalizing proverbial kind, it is tied for its point to the situation in which it is spoken, and when adrift from that situation may become unintelligible. Mark would seem here to be constructing a theory by which to assure his readers that any parables of Jesus there may be are secured in their application for the Church's needs by virtue of a private elucidation of them from apostolic lips. The direction taken by such application appears in the interpretation which is then given of the parable of the sower. It is generally agreed that this is to be attributed to the Church rather than to Jesus, on the score both of its treatment of the parable as an allegory and of its thought and specialized vocabulary. It reflects the Church's interests, and as Mark has used it and the sayings he attaches to it, those interests are missionary interests. The parable, which is said to be the key to the others, is made to refer to different kinds of Christians, and the secret of the kingdom is now shown to be this, that despite the failures and disappointments from those who become unfruitful in face of satanic opposition, persecution, and worldliness, the gospel is irresistible through those who produce its fruit abundantly, and who by refusing to conceal it receive from God's hands the full measure which they themselves have used, and because they come with hands full.

The discourse in 7. 1-23 is also a compilation by the evangelist. It begins with a sharply defined setting. Jesus is about to depart for heathen territory; on the one hand Pharisees and a deputation of scribes from Jerusalem, and on the other hand certain from among the number of Jesus' disciples who are in the habit of eating with defiled, that is unwashed, hands, which is here expanded into a contravention of the whole Jewish practice of ceremonial purity as such. The issue thus raised is not dealt with immediately but only later, when it has first been given a twist by Jesus' enunciation to a specially summoned audience that a man cannot be defiled by anything entering him from outside but only by what is already within, and when the disciples, who do not understand this because it is said to be a parable, are given a private interpretation of it to the effect that what goes into a man goes into the belly and not the heart. It is now evident that it is food and not unclean hands which is being talked about, and the implication of the statement is said to be (by an awkwardly appended participial clause) that Jesus has made all foods clean (7.19). The things inside a man which defile him are then given in a list of sins without parallel in the vocabulary of the gospels, but reminiscent of that of the epistles. In the middle section of the discourse, which connects the original issue of ritual purity with the tradition of the elders, the whole Jewish nation as such is condemned for its superficial reverence of God in holding to this tradition of human enactments as though it were divine doctrine. This condemnation is made by means of Isa. 29.13 in the Greek version, which alone makes the necessary point, and which, as Col. 2.22 shows, was used in Christian circles for scriptural denunciation of ritual asceticism. To this is added a section which could stand on its own, condemning evasion of the fifth commandment by the practice of Korban. Again it would seem that Mark, by this particular selection of material, and by his arrangement and adaptation of it, has slanted the tradition in the direction of a church of his own day which is at grips with the Gentile mission. He has in mind the conflicts within such a church between those for whom only a radical break with Judaism, its ceremonial purity, and its food regulations permitted them to be followers of the Lord into the world, and those who in one way or another remain tied to these things.

What we have then in these two chapters is not the gospel and its teachings themselves (which are taken for granted and nowhere stated) but rather results already brought about by the gospel and its teachings. This is so in other teaching sections also. Thus the gospel is not in itself eating with sinners, or feasting rather than fasting, or disregard of sabbath regulations and ceremonial purity, any more than it is in itself the refusal of divorce, the receiving of children, the renunciation of wealth, the rendering to Caesar and to God what belongs to them, or belief in resurrection. These are rather states of life and attitudes of mind and heart for which the gospel has been responsible, and by debates which are both positive and negative in character they are asserted and defended against what threatens them in the Church. Since behind these states and attitudes, and making them possible, lies a radical break with Judaism, though not the abandonment of its essence in the two great commandments, the principal opponents emerge as the ubiquitous Pharisees (though not so much as in the Gospels of Matthew and Luke), and above all the theological representatives of Judaism, the scribes. These are said pointedly to come down from Jerusalem (3. 22; 7.1), are alone denounced as a class (12.38ff), are in danger of the sin against the Holy Spirit (3. 22-30), and along with the Jerusalem priests and elders make up the group which finally secures the destruction of Jesus (8.31; 10.33; 11.27; 14.1,43,53; 15.1,31). It is noticeable that the replies to these opponents, like the private instructions of disciples, show evidence of the language of the later Church, and so speak to its situation; as when, for example, "Those who are whole have no need of a physician but those who are sick" is further explicated by "I came not to call the righteous but sinners" (2.17); or when the present feast time of the bridegroom with his attendants is modified by a subsequent fasting when he is taken away (2.20); or when the particular and dramatic "Behold my mother and my brethren" is generalized as "Whoever does the will of God, he is my brother and sister and mother" (3.35); or when the doctrine of external and internal is said to abolish food laws, (7.19); or when the controversy on divorce leads to a Church rule on the matter (10. 10-12); or when the incident of the rich man whose wealth is a barrier to discipleship is prolonged into an encouragement of those who have abandoned all for the gospel and Jesus. (10. 28-31).

In view of the specific occasions from which it emerges, and the largely controversial form in which it has been shaped in the tradition, the teaching in Mark's Gospel may properly be called a situation ethic; but the question then is, "What is the situation of which it is the ethic?" It may be a salutary exercise in reading any teaching passage in Mark's Gospel to consider whether it does not frequently gain its sharp point by reference to the situation in the church for which Mark was writing, or when seen as a means either of encouragement or criticism of that church by the use of its own tradition. We are here, as elsewhere in this Gospel, no longer at the beginning of things, and it looks as if this book in its particular compound of a teaching and a miracle tradition might best be regarded as an extended missionary pamphlet or vade-mecum.

4

THE PERSON AND
PASSION OF JESUS

There is a dictum of the nineteenth century German theologian
Martin Kähler which has gained wide currency, partly through
its popularization by Karl Barth, that "to state the matter
somewhat provocatively, one could call the gospels passion
naratives with extended introductions". This is one of those
piquant statements which can be highly suggestive while remaining basically false. On the one hand it directs the attention, as
Kähler intended, to the non-biographical character of the
gospels, and to the probability that they, or some of them,
emerged within Christian communities for whom, so far as we
can tell from the rest of the New Testament, the main accent
of the Christian message was on Christ crucified and risen. To
be a Christian was to have taken up a certain attitude towards
Christ's death and resurrection rather than towards his mighty
works or his teaching. So the form-critic is ready to advance the
hypothesis that the passion narrative, no doubt in a much shorter
form than now appears in the gospels, was from the first the
kernel of the gospel tradition and the earliest part of it to take
shape. This is a plausible hypothesis even if some arguments
adduced in support of it are dubious. Thus the appeal for proof
of it to the existence of several different yet closely similar
passion narratives depends on one particular reading of the
evidence whereby Luke's and John's passion narratives are
deemed to be independent of Mark's (as Matthew's plainly is

not), and it would lose its force if, as some hold, these are basically reproductions of Mark's with considerable additions to it and interpretation of it. And while it is the case that, in distinction from the remainder of the gospels, the passion narratives have more of the character of a single continuous story, thus suggesting an early formation, this is a matter of degree only, and they are still largely made up of individual units.

On the other hand Kähler's dictum is plainly untrue of Matthew's Gospel, where the passion narrative, a slavish reproduction of Mark's, is the final section of a book which is predominantly a composition of the teaching of Jesus. It is hardly true of Luke's, in which the emphasis is rather upon the life of Jesus and his resurrection as the transition to the life of the Church, or of John's, where the death of Jesus, in relation to his life, to the nation, and to the disciples, is so fully expounded before the passion begins. In Mark's Gospel the passion certainly casts a longer shadow back over the story, but the effect of frequent predictions of the passion and resurrection advanced into the body of the narrative (8.31ff; 9.31; 10.34ff), together with the glimpses of future glory in the Transfiguration and in the discourse of Chapter 13, is to place the reader well before the passion begins in a position to understand who Jesus is. The view that the gospels were, so to speak, written from the passion narrative backwards fails to do justice to the traditions of the acts and the teaching of Jesus in their own right, and seeks to arrive too easily at a unity both of the gospels in themselves, and of the gospels with the rest of the New Testament, by bringing them within a Pauline formula.

Yet Mark's Gospel as a single *euaggelion* presumably has a unity somewhere, and if it is to be found anywhere it is not in the tradition of the mighty works, nor in that of the teaching, nor in the passion, in themselves, nor in some combination of these, but rather in the christology, the presentation of the person of Jesus, whose works and teaching and passion they are. This is already hinted at in the mighty works as a whole, if they are rightly interpreted as his baptism of men in holy spirit and his defeat of the realm of evil. It is hinted at by some of them more particularly, as in the disclosure by the demons that he is "the Holy One of God" (1.24) or "the Son of the Most High God" (5.7), and in such questions as "What is this? He commands the unclean spirits and they obey him" (1.27), or "Who is this that the winds and the sea obey him?" (4.41); and it comes momentarily to the surface in the claim over the healing of the paralytic that "the Son of man has power on earth to forgive sins" (2.10). It is insinuated also by the teaching as a whole in its form of a constant successful conflict with the religious leaders. It is indicated more particularly by the statement that "he taught with authority and not as the scribes" (1.21) and by the absoluteness of his disposition of, and judgement upon, the concerns of the Jewish religion, including the Old Testament; and it comes momentarily to the surface in the claim that "the Son of man is lord of the sabbath" (2.28). It is also hinted at in the existence of disciples detached by his summons from all ties of possessions and kin, and who not only receive his instruction but align themselves with his destiny by "following" him, a word used in this sense of attachment to a person nowhere in the New Testament outside the gospels. What is hinted at in these ways is, however, made explicit by a certain skeleton framework of stories about Jesus—his baptism at the beginning, his transfiguration in the middle, and his trial and death at the end—which articulate the narrative, and by certain expressions of Jesus about himself which thread its latter part.

We are here concerned particularly with three appellations, "the Christ", "the Son of man" and "the Son of God", and especially with the last two. The first, "the Christ", appears at two important points, that is, at Peter's confession in the name of the disciples that Jesus is the Christ in contrast to various judgements of men upon him (8.27ff), and in the question of the high priest, "Art thou the Christ?", to which Jesus is represented as answering in the affirmative (14.61f). It fails, however, to carry weight, for in the first case it is followed by

65

one of the Markan injunctions to silence, and in the second it is glossed by an additional title "the Son of the Blessed One". Moreover in both contexts it is, as it were, immediately replaced by the term "the Son of man"—in the first by the announcement of his necessary suffering, and in the second of his future glory and coming. It is thus suggested that "the Christ" is by itself unsatisfactory and needs further definition, and that the question whether Jesus is the Christ can only be answered by a "Yes, but. . . ." Indeed, the opening words of Mark's book, "The beginning of the gospel of Jesus Christ", show that by the time of writing, as elsewhere in the New Testament, the term had lost its original meaning of the future anointed king in the divine kingdom (12.35; 13.21; 15.32), and had become a further proper name for Jesus. For that reason the only other instance of its use by Mark in the saying "whoever gives you a cup of water to drink because you bear the name of Christ" (9.41) cannot in that form be a genuine utterance of Jesus.

The weight then lies on "the Son of man" and "the Son of God". An assessment of these terms is, however, beset with acute critical and historical problems, and requires from the ordinary modern reader an initial revolution in his thinking. When at the Council of Chalcedon in the fifth century the Church arrived at its classical formulation of the person of Christ in the doctrine of his two natures, his godhead and manhood, a decisive document in the discussion was the Tome of Pope Leo I, in which the two natures were set forth in language of this kind: "Each nature in common with the other performs the function proper to it, the Word performing what belongs to the Word, and the flesh carrying out what belongs to the flesh. The one sparkles with miracles, the other succumbs to injuries. For—a fact which must be repeated again and again—one and the same person is truly Son of God and truly Son of man." Leo was here using language with which Christians had been familiar probably from early in the second century. As Son of God Jesus was divine, as Son of man he was human. "To state the matter somewhat provocatively", in Kähler's phrase, one might say that in Mark's Gospel it is the other way round. Though not altogether true it would be approximately true to say that here when it is required to emphasize the humanity of Jesus he is called the Son of God, and that when it is required to state the equivalent of our word "divinity" (for the gospels do not have the word or the idea) then he is called the Son of man.

This is not the place to attempt to treat in detail of this seemingly innocent appellation "the Son of man", upon which there is a veritable spate of literature which shows no sign of abating. There are a few facts which can be simply stated. The term is found in the New Testament only once outside the gospels (on the lips of Stephen, Acts 7. 56), from which may perhaps be deduced that it fell early out of the Christian vocabulary, and played little part in the later development of Christian thinking about Jesus. In the gospels it is found some eighty times, and is found in all their various strata, but never in narrative and (with one exception, in St. John's Gospel) always on the lips of Jesus, from which it may probably be deduced that despite its early disappearance it could not be dislodged from the gospel tradition that Jesus had used it of himself and that no one else had used it of him. Fourteen of these instances are in Mark's Gospel, and are distributed as follows The first two (2.10, 28) occur within conflict stories (the first somewhat awkwardly), and refer to Jesus in his exercise of the divine prerogative of the forgiveness of sins and of authority over the divine ordinance of the sabbath. The rest stretch from Chapters 8 to 14, and not only punctuate the narrative, but play a considerable part in carrying it forward. Among them are three self-contained predictions by Jesus, in greater or less detail, of his coming rejection as the Son of man by the authorities, his death at their hands, and his subsequent resurrection, and these may well have been later formulations of the Church in the light of the events (8. 31; 9. 31; 10. 33f). There are similar predictions elsewhere of this coming suffering, one introduced somewhat awkwardly into a conversation about the return of Elijah ("How is it written of the Son of man that he must suffer many things and be set at nought?" 9.12), one as an extension of the prophecy of betrayal ("The Son of man goes as is it written of him, but woe to the man by whom the Son of man is betrayed" 14.21), and one as a transition from the scene in Gethsemane to the arrest ("The hour is come; behold the Son of man is handed over into the hands of sinners" 14.41). At 10.45 a saying, which is supplementary in its context, unites the earthly ministry of Jesus and his redemptive suffering as being of one piece, and could be understood as referring to both as already past ("The Son of man came not to be ministered to but to minister, and to give his life a ransom for many"). At 9.7 the future resurrection of the Son of man is mentioned in one of the mysterious Markan injunctions to silence, in this case silence about what the three disciples had seen at the Transfiguration. The remaining three instances are eschatological, namely, the prophecy of the coming of the Son of man on the clouds with great power and glory to gather his elect as the final event of the apocalyptic drama in Chapter 13 (13.26); the prophecy, in reply to the high priest's question, that his interlocutors will see the Son of man sitting at the right hand of power and coming with the clouds of heaven (14.62); and finally a saying, which is relatively isolated in its context, uniting the earthly ministry of Jesus with this eschatological future ("Whoever is ashamed of me and my words [or "and mine"] in this adulterous and sinful age, the Son of man will be ashamed of him when he comes in the glory of his father with the holy angels" (8.38).

What is the tenor of statements so constructed as to have "the Son of man" as the subject of the verb? Just as the sentence "The Young Pretender has arrived" would have had an added force compared with the sentence "Charles Edward Stuart has arrived", so the sentence 'The Son of man is passing by" would have something additional to the sentence "Jesus of Nazareth is passing by", especially if the speaker appears to be referring to himself in the third person. What is this additional something?

That would depend on the content of the term "the Son of man", but since the term is simply introduced without any explanation this content has to be deduced from the sentences themselves and from any suggestions about the origin and provenance of the term. Here all is obscure and hotly debated. In Greek the phrase without the definite article ("a son of the man") is untranslatable; with the definite article ("the son of the man") it is unintelligible, prompting the question, "which son of which man are we talking about?" It only begins to be intelligible as the Greek rendering of an intractably semitic idiom, in which "son of" means "belonging to", and "son of man" means one of the human species, a synonym for man, as in the parallelism: "What is man, that thou art mindful of him? And the son of man that thou visitest him?" (Ps. 8.4). Whatever else it may come to mean it can never leave behind this basic sense of humanity. It is used very frequently in the book of Ezekiel as the mode of God's address to the prophet, but this throws little light on the usage of the gospels. There is, however, one Old Testament passage which certainly lies behind it, and which is echoed in the gospels, Daniel's vision of the night in which he saw "with the clouds of heaven one like a son of man was coming, and to the Ancient of days [namely, God] he came; and was presented before him; and to him was given dominion, glory, and sovereignty, with all peoples and nations and tongues serving him; his dominion an everlasting dominion not to pass away, and his sovereignty not to be destroyed" (Dan. 7.13ff). Later in the same chapter of Daniel this figure of one like a son of man is revealed to be an ideogram of a corporate body, the saints of the Most High, the faithful Israelites who have remained loyal under persecution (Dan. 7.21ff).

Is this the immediate background, and is there a straight carry over from Daniel to the gospels, so that the Son of man is the true Israel, and hence the true man, to be identified first perhaps with Jesus and his disciples, but in the last resort with Jesus alone, whose rejection and suffering are thus asserted to

69

be divinely decreed as written in Daniel, and are equally due for vindication as the means to the establishment of God's kingdom? Daniel's vision, however, does not of itself yield the specific title "the Son of man", but only the basis for such. Is there evidence that the one might have developed into the other by subsequent reflection? The only surviving evidence is in the Jewish apocryphal book, I Enoch, which is itself the subject of debate, since it is known so far chiefly in later (15th-16th cent.) Ethiopic translations of a Greek version of a semitic original, and the question whether it is pre-Christian or post-Christian remains open, especially as the relevant section of the book has not yet turned up in the library of the Qumran community. This is a special section called the Similitudes (Chapters 37-71), in which there appears alongside God, and as occupying his throne, an individual figure called "the (this, that) Son of man". He is introduced (Chapter 46) in terms clearly derived from Daniel Chapter 7, and is then depicted as the world's judge, as the possessor of righteousness and wisdom, as the revealer of mysteries in bringing to light both righteousness and sin, and as the champion and rewarder of the righteous elect. Is the greater precision in I Enoch of this supra-terrestrial figure, who belongs with God but is still called by the name of man, the product of a theological development of Daniel's vision, assisted perhaps by a more widely current religious concept of a heavenly man, and did this development take place in some possibly restricted (Galilean?) circle within Judaism? Is it some already established usage which accounts for the curious feature that in using it Jesus must appear either to be referring to himself for some reason in the third person, or to be speaking about someone else? Is its purpose to assert the ultimate character of Jesus—of his acts, which include the divine prerogative of the forgiveness of sins and the control of a divine ordinance such as the sabbath; of his words, which are to remain when all else has perished (13.31); of his death as the final death? If so its force will lie, at least partly, in the height of paradox which is reached when the one who is handed over (by God) to men for their scrutiny and rejection as counterfeit (this is the meaning of the verb used in Mark 8.31) is the one whose divinely ordained function is to scrutinize all men as their judge when they are handed over to him for final acceptance or rejection. Are all three uses of the term—for Jesus' earthly ministry, for his suffering, and for his future glory—authentic? or has one or other of them been attached to him later, either in the light of past events or in the light of Christian hope for the future, and at a time when perhaps the title was already on its way to become, like "the Christ", another name for Jesus? These are all questions to which there does not seem to be the possibility of a definite answer, and not the least surprising feature of this surprising Gospel is that so much of what it wishes to convey about its central figure should hang upon a term which died so early a death and whose remains are so difficult to decipher.

At certain points the term "the Son of man" passes over into the term "the Son of God", as when the prophecy of the coming of the Son of man in power is followed by the assertion that no one knows the time of it, not even the angels, nor the Son, but the Father only (13. 26-32); or when, in the course of a single sentence, it is said that whoever is ashamed of Jesus and his words now, the Son of man will be ashamed of him when he comes in the glory of his father with the holy angels (8.38). Father and son are correlative terms, and the Father is father not of the Son of man but of the Son (of God). What is intended by the application of this term to Jesus? If a difficulty of Son of man is its obscurity, due possibly to its lying on a precise but no longer recoverable background and to its having had a restricted meaning, a difficulty about the term "Son of God" is that it had the widest possible background in the religious thought of the time, and could mean far too much. The fruits of Zeus's amorous adventures, the gods as his offspring, semi-divine heroes like Heracles, the divinities of the mystery cults, and even the Roman emperor, were all called sons of God. This pagan usage even finds expression in Mark's Gospel at the point where the evangelist chooses to record that the centurion at the Cross, speaking as a representative of the Gentile world and perhaps as a symbol of the future Gentile Church, makes a kind of confession of faith within his own terminology, and affirms at the moment of Jesus' death, "Truly this man was a son of God". Once more the definite article is important, for only with it does the phrase begin to be a disciplined one—the single Son of the one God. Its use in the gospels only begins to be intelligible when it is seen to be a rendering of another semitic idiom, according to which "son of" means not "belonging to", nor even primarily "the physical offspring of", but the special object of a father's regard, who owes his father obedience and is to reproduce his character. In the Old Testament Israel, as a people which has been redeemed by God and which knows his will through the Law, is called the Son of God. Whether the title was used of the messiah in first century Judaism is a matter of debate. If it was so, this is likely to have been through the medium of Ps. 2.7, where God appoints the Davidic king with the words, 'Thou art my son, this day have I begotten thee", which itself probably rests on the prophecy of Nathan in 2 Sam. 7.14, in which God says of the Davidic king, "I will be to him a father, and he shall be to me a son", a passage which is found interpreted of the future Davidic king-messiah in the Qumran literature.

Even if the words "Son of God" are to be omitted on textual grounds from the opening words of Mark's Gospel they would not be out of place there. Although the title is used with great reserve by Mark [1] the points at which, and the manner in which, it is used are highly significant. Firstly (as an attestation of who Jesus is) it is found, apart from the centurion's own version of it, not on human but only on supernatural lips. Thus at the initial episode of the baptism, when Jesus receives the Spirit for his

[1] As is also the word "Father" of God—used once of the Father of the Son of man (8. 38), once as the Father of the Son (13. 32), once in the prayer of Jesus to God (14. 36), and once of God as the Father of the disciples (11. 25); but this last may be an interpolation from Matthew's Gospel.

work, he is declared by a voice from heaven (i.e. by God) to be his beloved (= only) Son, on whom his pleasure rests. At the Transfiguration, which initiates the second part of the Gospel, the heavenly voice is heard again, this time for the benefit of the disciples, "This is my beloved Son", to which is added the command, "listen to him" (9.7). Otherwise it is only the demons who so address him, and for this reason are reduced to silence (3.11; 5.7). It is the supernatural world alone which knows Jesus to be Son of God. Secondly, it is predominantly in the context of his testing, and of the trial of his human obedience, that he is so addressed, or that he himself speaks and acts as such. Thus he is first declared Son of God at the moment when he has undergone along with sinners a baptism of repentance. The heavily symbolic story of the Transfiguration is unique in the gospels in that here alone the status of Jesus in his future glory is depicted in the quasi-physical terms of a temporary metamorphosis of his body and clothing by the divine radiance, but in Mark's context the additional words of the heavenly voice, "listen to him", are made to refer back to the teaching which Jesus has now begun to give on the necessity of the humiliation and suffering of the Son of man and on the necessity of the cross for the disciple (8. 31-37); moreover the incident is followed by a passionate outburst at the constraint under which he is compelled to live and work, "O faithless generation, how long shall I be with you, how long shall I bear with you"? (9.19). So also in his own use of it a real ignorance is said to be involved in being the Son, who must leave the certain knowledge of the future in the hands of the Father (13.32). In Gethsemane the Son is seen addressing God as "Abba, Father" in the context of a final testing, which involves a desperate human agony of faith and prayer and a struggle without parallel in the Gospel for the consecration of the will to obedience. The suffering of the Son of man is something determined as it were externally by the will of God, and Jesus is propelled towards it by Scripture. Its inner moral meaning is the obedience of the Son of God in his humanity.

Mark's story moves in Chapters 14-15 to the actual narration of this previously predicted and interpreted death of the Son of man, but it does so only through the gateway of the long discourse of Chapter 13. Here, in reply to a double question from four disciples, which itself arises from a previous prophecy by Jesus of the complete destruction of the temple, he warns them not to be deceived by those who will come in his name with impressive claims, nor to be disturbed by wars, disturbances, and famines, which are not themselves the end but only the beginning of woes; he prophesies that in the pursuit of the gospel they will be arraigned before the courts, when they are to rely on the Holy Spirit in defence, and that in the fratricidal strife which will break out they will be universally hated and will attain salvation only by final endurance; he commands them, when they see Daniel's "abomination which makes desolate" standing as a personal figure where he should not, to flee Judea instantly, since the oppression then to break out will be the worst the world will ever have seen, and will be such as would destroy the whole human race did not God curtail it for the sake of the elect (who are to beware of the seduction of false prophets and messianic pretenders at that time); he announces that after this oppression, and along with the dissolution of the natural order, the Son of man will be seen coming on the clouds with great power and glory to gather the whole elect; and he closes with two parables, of the fig tree and the man who goes abroad, the first as an assurance that this coming with its premonitory signs will take place in their time, and the second as an exhortation to constant watchfulness, since no one but the Father knows the day or the hour of it.

This chapter is unique in the gospel. It resembles 4. 1-34 and 7. 1-23 in being a discourse made up of separate units and sayings on a common subject, but, to a far greater extent than they, it is a unified and consecutive whole, concerned with a single theme—"these things" (verses 4, 8, 29): "all these things" (verse 30) and is articulated by notes of sequence (verses 7, 8, 10, 14, 21, 24, 26, 27). This does not prevent the chapter from

74

being, both as a whole and in its parts, the most problematic in the book, as may be seen from the review of over a century's debate on it in Dr G. R. Beasley-Murray's study, *Jesus and the Future*. Thus there are internal contradictions, as between the statement that all will happen in the present generation with warning signs (28ff) and the statement that no one knows the day or hour so that watch must be made for what comes un-expectedly (32ff); or between the disciples as arrested during the Gentile mission (9ff) and as being still in Judea to see the abomination (14ff). Moreover the prophecy as a whole is not an answer to the original question about the date of the destruction of the temple. The attempts to make it such by the addition of a further question about the date of the final con-summation ("What is the sign of the consummation of all these things?" 13.4), and by the identification of the temple's desecration by the abomination with its destruction, are artificial. The chapter is rightly called "apocalypse", since it is in outline an unveiling to an esoteric group of the final events, largely in the traditional Old Testament and post-Old Testament language for such things; but it is apocalypse with a difference, since a great part of it is not descriptive and in the third person, but is directed to the disciples in the second person plural as warning, advice, and exhortation. These two types of statement have been separated out, and various theories advanced as to their origin and previous unity, including the theory that Mark has used an already current Jewish apocalypse and has interpolated it with Christian material.

On these grounds of the problematic character of the chapter and of its concentrated apocalyptic content the tension between the modern reader and the evangelist is likely to be at its greatest here, but this must not be allowed to obscure the fact that this discourse was of crucial importance to Mark in the construction of his Gospel. Before narrating the Lord's passion he has here composed what amounts to the Lord's farewell discourse to his disciples and his last word to men. Jesus is here represented as speaking as if from beyond the dissolution of all things with the knowledge and authority of the one who is alone privy to the final mysteries of the divine dispensation of the world ("Behold, I have told you all things in advance," 13.22); "heaven and earth shall pass away, but my words shall not pass away" (13.31), and as speaking not simply in the past, but so directly to the present that for a moment the group of listening disciples is forgotten, and it is the reader of the Gospel who is addressed by the exalted Lord ("let the reader understand", 13.14). It is the reader who is here being warned to distinguish the wars and disturbances traditionally associated in the Old Testament with the end from the end itself, and is being told that he will be living at the beginning of the end-events themselves once he sees the appearance of the Antichrist figure, from whom and his attendant false prophets and messianic pretenders he is to flee instantly. With its final impressive words, "What I say to you I say to all, Watch!", the discourse, and indeed the whole Gospel, reaches out to its maximum possible audience.

It is the thesis of the German scholar W. Marxsen (*Der Evangelist Markus* 1959) that all this, and especially Mark's identification of the apocalyptic "abomination of desolation" with the destruction of the temple, must be taken as a clear indication of the precise occasion and purpose of the writing of the Gospel. The occasion is the advance of the Roman armies through Galilee upon Jerusalem in A.D. 66, when, according to Eusebius (*Eccl. Hist.* III. 5. 3) "the people of the church in Jerusalem had been commanded by an oracle, vouchsafed to approved men there before the war, to leave the city and to dwell in a certain town of Perea named Pella". The purpose is either to command this flight or to approve of it, and to interpret for a Palestinian Christian community or communities the times in which they were living. This thesis would perhaps be strengthened if it were taken along with another thesis of the French scholar, E. Trocmé (*La Formation de l'Evangile selon Marc* 1963), that the original version of Mark's Gospel ended with Chapter 13, and that Chapters 14-15 are additions of a later reviser. In either case, however, it would be difficult to see what purpose the previous twelve chapters were supposed to serve. In its position in the Gospel as we have it, as a prelude to the passion narrative, Chapter 13 reiterates more powerfully than any previous statements and predictions that the death of Jesus is the final tribulation, the death of the Son of man, which secures both the judgement and the redemption of the world, and which promises for the disciples both an extremity of tribulation and an ultimate deliverance.

But it was of the essence of the Christian gospel that the tribulation which the Lord had initiated he had first himself undergone. Mark's account of this tribulation of Jesus in his passion narrative exhibits on the whole remarkable brevity. It also bristles with difficulties, since it is constructed largely from separate units in whose formation Christian theological and devotional interests have been so strong as to make an accurate reconstruction of the events or of the human motives involved virtually impossible. The bare skeleton of any passion narrative will be an account of the arrest of Jesus, of his trial and condemnation, and of his death and burial. The fact that there are two trials, one before the Sanhedrin, the official representatives of the Jewish people, and one before the Roman governor, was presumably due to the fact that Judea was an occupied country, though the question whether the Jews were permitted the capital penalty under Roman rule is much debated. The gospels differ in the place they assign to the Jewish and the Roman sides of the affair. In Mark the weight falls heavily on the Jewish side, which is described at some length. At a meeting at an improbable hour on Passover night an attempt to incriminate Jesus over something he had said about the temple proved unsuccessful through the incompetence of suborned witnesses. He is then condemned for blasphemy on the score of his acknowledgement that he is the messiah, the Son of the Blessed One, and his assertion that they will see the Son of man seated at the right hand of power and coming on the clouds of heaven (though it is not evident from Jewish sources that any of this would have constituted blasphemy). By contrast, the proceedings before Pilate are perfunctory in the extreme—simply the unexplained question out of the blue, "Are you the king of the Jews?" and the non-committal reply, "You say it". Then follows at far greater length the highly irregular offer by the governor of a choice between Jesus and the brigand Barabbas. This may be a continuation of the question asked by Jesus at his arrest, "Have you come out as against a brigand to take me?" and behind both may lie the scriptural sentence, "He was reckoned with the lawless ones" (Isa. 53.12). Jesus is then mocked as a dummy king, and is led away to crucifixion. Thus in Mark's account the death of Jesus is a Jewish affair though carried out by Roman instrumentality, and is an extended version of the statement of Peter in his speech at Pentecost, "You [Jews] used heathen men to crucify and kill him" (Acts 2.23).

From this point the story moves rapidly, and is almost intolerably unadorned and realistic. Jesus is completely alone and entirely bereft of human sympathy and contact. In fulfilment of his own predictions (14. 27-30) all the disciples have forsaken him and fled (14.50) and Peter has denied him, denied that he knows who he is, and denied that he knows what his questioners are talking about (14. 66-72). Now everyone who passes by the cross, including the chief priests and scribes, mock him, as do those who are crucified with him (15. 29-32). There is darkness over the land for three hours. Jesus, who has spoken only two sentences since his arrest, in his replies to the high priest and to Pilate, speaks now for a third and last time with the cry, "My God, my God, why has thou forsaken me?", and then dies.

This bare skeleton Mark clothes with certain material of an interpretative and didactic kind, mostly intended to show Jesus as being in control of each situation and as offering the key to it. This begins with the moving episode of the anointing of Jesus on the head by an unnamed woman, which was possibly meant to be an anointing of him as king messiah, but which

78

Jesus relates to his death by interpreting it as an advance embalming for burial. The Passover meal is prepared by an arrangement which falls out exactly according to his prevision. Nothing however is said about the meal itself except that at it he prophesies his betrayal by one of those present, and then, in language probably already formed within the liturgical tradition of Mark's church, blesses and breaks bread for the disciples and relates it to his own body, or self, and blesses wine for their drinking, and defines it as his blood of the covenant shed for many. It is thus suggested that his death is to be the inaugural sacrifice of a covenant between God and mankind, in which the disciples are included by their solidarity in and with his own person; but the meal also looks forward to the messianic banquet in the kingdom of God (14.25). On leaving the meal Jesus prophesies that all will take offence at him, but assures them that this will be reversed when, after resurrection, he goes before them into Galilee. He predicts the threefold denial of Peter, and this is subsequently recorded in detail, both in order to show the prediction fulfilled and, probably, as a warning to Christians of the peril of apostasy. Then in Gethsemane, in the context of a theme which is often found as a didactic motif in the epistles, the theme of sleeping and waking, Jesus himself enters into the real trial of which the human tribunals will be but a shadow, and from which he enjoins the three unheeding disciples to pray to be delivered. The language used is vehement. Jesus is said to be distraught with anxiety and in utter bewilderment, and the cup which he had previously assured two of his disciples that they would drink with him (10.39) he now begs the Father to remove, but with the qualification that the Father's will be done. It is here suggested that the inner meaning of his death, and what makes it a sacrifice of a covenant between God and men, is the obedience of the Son to the Father in the weakness but willingness of his humanity, and in the surrender of his will in an agony of faith and prayer at the contemplation of ultimate dissolution.

The narrative contains two further interpretative features.

The first is the use of Old Testament language. Only once is a scriptural passage expressly cited, when (14.27) the desertion of the disciples is said to fulfil the words in Zech. 13.7, "Smite the shepherd and the sheep shall be scattered", while the arrest is said to take place that the scriptures in general may be fulfilled (14.49). The story, however, is full of Old Testament echoes. Thus the words at the last supper "the blood of the covenant" recall Exodus 24.8 or Zechariah 9.11; the prophecy of betrayal recalls Psalm 41.9; the words of agony in Gethsemane "My soul is exceedingly sorrowful to the point of death" are from a single psalm (42.6, 11; cf. Ps. 43.5); the false witnesses recall Psalm 35.11; the reply to the high priest combines Psalm 110.1 and Daniel 7.13; the spitting, buffeting, and blows of the high priest's servants and the demand to play the prophet (14.65) rest upon the words of Isaiah 50.6 where the prophet says "I gave my back to the smiters and my cheeks to them that plucked off the hair; I hid not my face from shame and spitting". The parting of the garments, the wagging of the head of those who mock at the cross, and the cry of dereliction are from Psalm 22.1,7,18; the draught of vinegar from Psalm 69.21; and the women watching from a distance reflect Psalm 38.11, "My lovers and my friends stand aloof from my plague". The stress on the silence of Jesus may also rest upon Isaiah 53.7, "He opened not his mouth." Here Mark may be writing less as an individual author than as a representative of a church's already interpreted tradition. The purpose of this use of Old Testament language is to say that the passion is neither historical accident nor personal tragedy but the action of God himself, even though it is also the action of the will of Jesus. Here is again an extended version of Peter's statement at Pentecost that "he was given up to you by the deliberate plan and will of God" (Acts 2.23).

The second feature is that the temple moves into the centre of the picture. Immediately after the triumphal entry Jesus surveys the temple, and on the next day, after cursing the fig tree as a symbol of barren Judaism, cleanses the temple, and, it may be, by forbidding anyone to carry a vessel through it, intends to stop sacrificial worship altogether (11.16). Although scripture is here quoted to the effect that the temple is to become a house of prayer for all the nations, this cannot refer to the present temple now reformed by Jesus, since at the opening of the discourse of Chapter 13 Jesus prophesies its destruction beyond recall. As the first charge in his trial before the Sanhedrin it is alleged that he had said, "I will destroy this temple made with hands and in three days I will build another not made with hands", (14.58) and these words are thrown in Jesus' teeth by those who mock him on the cross (15.29). Here Mark is at his most enigmatic, one might almost say his most infuriating; for if Jesus said this, or something like this, it would perhaps be the most revolutionary thing he ever did say, and would suggest that the positive side of his destructive judgement on Jerusalem and Judaism was to be the erection in a new mode of all that the temple had stood for. But what he did say we cannot know for, Mark says, it was the allegation of witnesses who were false, and who in any case could not agree on what had been said. Finally at the moment of Jesus' death comes the highly symbolic statement that the veil of the temple was rent from top to bottom. The function of the veil was to conceal the presence of God from the eyes of men. Now through the death of the obedient Son all that hides God from men is taken away, and God tabernacles among men. Significantly therefore at this point the centurion, as a representative of the Gentile world, utters his confession of faith, "Truly this man was a son of God". Here the theme of the temple reaches its end. In the centurion's acknowledgement of the Sonship of Jesus at his death the implication of the words at the cleansing of the temple comes to light. In the body of Christ, crucified and risen, there is a house of prayer to God for all the Gentiles.

We are thus brought back again to the enigmatic ending of Mark's Gospel. The other gospels end with an account not only of the appearances of the risen Lord but also of the apostolic mission to the world to which he commissions the disciples.

Mark's Gospel should be judged by reference only to itself and not to other gospels, but the question remains whether the mission of the gospel to the world is not the content of Mark 16.1-18. At 14.27, in the context of a prophecy of the smiting of the shepherd and the scattering of his flock, Jesus had said: "After I am raised up I will go before you into Galilee". Here the resurrection is in parenthesis, and leads to something beyond itself. This something beyond is reiterated in the message of the young man at the tomb: "He goes before you into Galilee; there you will see him". Is this "going before" the going of a shepherd at the head of his flock, and is the meaning that Jesus, having "gone before", or led, his disciples from Galilee to Jerusalem (10.32ff), recovers them from their apostasy by his resurrection, and is now leading them out to the Gentile world? Perhaps so, perhaps not.

Critical studies of the gospels were responsible in the early years of this century for two dogmas which became widely current and influential—that Mark's Gospel is an account of the beginnings of Christianity, and that Christianity is essentially a simple gospel. It now appears that these two views cannot be held together, for if Mark's Gospel represents the beginnings of things Christianity cannot possibly be simple, and if Christianity is essentially simple Mark's Gospel cannot represent its beginnings Both dogmas are probably heresies.

APPENDIX

As these lectures were introductory in character, and were delivered to a non-specialist audience, the reader may care to know what is available in English for further study by way of commentaries, special studies, and articles on St Mark's Gospel. Some of the special studies and articles presume a knowledge of Greek, but may often be used by those with little or no knowledge of it. References to the principal foreign literature on the subject will be found in some of the English works.

The following abbreviations are used in the Bibliography

B.J.R.L.	*Bulletin of the John Rylands Library*
C.B.Q.	*Catholic Biblical Quarterly*
C.Q.R.	*Church Quarterly Review*
E.T.	*Expository Times*
H.T.R.	*Harvard Theological Review*
J.B.R.	*Journal of Biblical Religion*
J.B.L.	*Journal of Biblical Literature*
J.T.S.	*Journal of Theological Studies*
N.T.S.	*New Testament Studies*
S.J.T.	*Scottish Journal of Theology*
Z.N.W.	*Zeitschrift für die neutestamentliche Wissenschaft*

Bibliography

A. COMMENTARIES

1. ON THE ENGLISH TEXT

B. H. Branscomb. *The Gospel of Mark* (Moffatt New Testament Commentary). Hodder and Stoughton, 1952.

F. C. Grant. *The Gospel according to St Mark* (Interpreter's Bible, Vol. VII). Abingdon Press, 1951.

S. E. Johnson. *The Gospel according to St Mark* (Black's New Testament Commentaries). A. & C. Black, 1963.

C. F. D. Moule. *Mark* (Cambridge Bible Commentary). Cambridge University Press, 1965.

D. E. Nineham. *Saint Mark* (Pelican Gospel Commentaries). Penguin Books, 1963.

A. E. J. Rawlinson. *The Gospel according to St Mark* (Westminster Commentaries). Methuen, 1949.

C. H. Turner. *The Gospel according to St Mark* (in *A New Commentary on Holy Scripture,* ed. C. Gore, H. L. Goudge, and A. Guillaume). S.P.C.K., 1928.

R. Mcl. Wilson. *Mark* (in *Peake's Commentary on the Bible,* ed. M. Black and H. H. Rowley). Thomas Nelson, 1962.

2. ON THE GREEK TEXT

C. E. B. Cranfield. *The Gospel according to St Mark* (The Cambridge Greek Testament Commentary). Cambridge University Press, 1955.

V. Taylor. *The Gospel according to St Mark.* Macmillan, 1952.

B. STUDIES

1. GENERAL
(IN WHOLE OR IN PART
ON ST MARK'S GOSPEL)

F. W. Beare. *The Earliest Records of Jesus. A Companion to Huck's Synopsis,* S.P.C.K., 1962.

E. Best. *The Temptation and the Passion: The Markan Soteriology.* Cambridge University Press, 1965.

J. Bowman. *The Gospel of Mark.* The New Christian Jewish Passover Haggadah. E. J. Brill, 1965.

R. Bultmann. *The History of the Synoptic Tradition*. Blackwell, 1963.

T. A. Burkill. *Mysterious Revelation*. An Examination of the Philosophy of St Mark's Gospel. Cornell University Press, 1963.

P. Carrington. *The Primitive Christian Calendar*. A Study in the Making of the Marcan Gospel. Vol. I. Introduction and Text. Cambridge University Press, 1960.

—— *According to Mark*. A Running Commentary on the Oldest Gospel. Cambridge University Press, 1960.

M. Dibelius. *From Tradition to Gospel*. Ivor Nicholson and Watson, 1934.

A. M. Farrer. *A Study in St Mark*. Dacre Press, 1951.

—— *St Matthew and St Mark*. Dacre Press, 1954.

F. C. Grant. *The Earliest Gospel*. Studies in the evangelic tradition at its point of crystallization in writing. Abingdon Press, 1962 (r.p.)

—— *The Gospels, their Origin and Growth*. Faber, 1959.

H. A. Guy. *The Origin of the Gospel of Mark*. Hodder and Stoughton, 1954.

W. L. Knox. *The Sources of the Synoptic Gospels*. Vol. I, St Mark. Cambridge University Press, 1953.

R. H. Lightfoot. *The Gospel Message of St Mark*. Clarendon Press, 1950.

—— *History and Interpretation in the Gospels*. Hodder and Stoughton, 1935.

—— *Locality and Doctrine in the Gospels*. Hodder and Stoughton,1938.

E. Lohse. *Mark's Witness to Jesus Christ*. Lutterworth, 1955

J. H. Ropes. *The Synoptic Gospels*. Second Impression, Oxford University Press, 1960.

N. B. Stonehouse. *The Witness of Matthew and Mark to Christ*. Tyndale Press, 1944.

2. SPECIAL
(IN WHOLE OR IN PART ON ASPECTS OF ST MARK'S GOSPEL)

G. R. Beasley-Murray. *Jesus and the Future*. An Examination of the Criticism of the Eschatological Discourse, Mark 13, with special reference to the Little Apocalypse Theory. Macmillan, 1954.

—— *A Commentary on Mark Thirteen.* Macmillan, 1957.

G. H. Boobyer. *St Mark and the Transfiguration Story.* T. & T. Clark, 1942.

M. D. Hooker. *The Son of Man in Mark.* S.P.C.K., 1967.

U. Mauser. *Christ in the Wilderness.* The Wilderness Theme in the Second Gospel and its Basis in the Biblical Tradition. S.C.M. Press, 1963.

G. Neville. *The Advent Hope.* A Study in the Context of Mark XIII. Darton, Longman and Todd, 1961.

J. M. Robinson. *The Problem of History in Mark.* S.C.M. Press, 1957.

P. Winter. *The Trial of Jesus.* Walter de Gruyter, 1961.

J. E. Yates. *The Spirit and the Kingdom.* S.P.C.K., 1963.

C. ARTICLES IN JOURNALS
OR IN COMPOSITE WORKS

J. A. Allan. "The Gospel of the Son of God Crucified." *Interpretation,* 9 (1955).

C. K. Barrett. *The Background of Mark 10: 45.* New Testament Essays; Studies in Memory of Thomas Walter Manson. ed. A. J. B. Higgins. Manchester University Press, 1959.

C. Bonner. "Traces of Thaumaturgical Technique in the Miracles." *H.T.R.,* 20 (1927).

G. H. Boobyer. "The Secrecy Motif in St Mark's Gospel." *N.T.S.* 6 (1960).

—— "The Redaction of Mark IV. 1-34." *N.T.S.* 8 (1961).

—— "Galilee and the Galileans in St Mark's Gospel." *B.J.R.L.* 35 (1952-3).

—— "The Miracles of the Loaves and the Gentiles in St Mark's Gospel." *S.J.T.,* 6 (1953).

—— "The Eucharistic Interpretation of the Miracles of the Loaves in St Mark's Gospel." *J.T.S.* (n.s.), 3 (1952).

S. G. F. Brandon. *The Apologetical Factor in the Markan Gospel.* Studia Evangelica, Vol. II; Part I, The New Testament Scriptures. Ed. F. L. Cross. Akademie-Verlag, Berlin, 1964.

—— "The Date of the Markan Gospel." *N.T.S.,* 7 (1960-1).

W. E. Bundy. *Dogma and Drama in the Gospel of Mark.* New Testament Studies; Critical Essays in New Testament Interpretation. ed. E. P. Booth. Abingdon-Cokesbury Press, 1942.

T. A. Burkill. "The Notion of Miracle with special reference to S. Mark's Gospel." *Z.N.W.*, 50 (1959).

—— "The Hidden Son of Man in St Mark's Gospel." *Z.N.W.* 52 (1961).

H. B. Carré. *The Literary Structure of the Gospel of Mark.* Studies in Early Christianity. Ed. S. J. Case. The Century Co., 1928.

R. P. Casey. "St Mark's Gospel." *Theology,* lv (1952).

C. P. Ceroke. "Is Mark 2. 10 a Saying of Jesus?" *C.B.Q.*, 22. (1960).

C. E. B. Cranfield. "The Baptism of our Lord. A Study of S. Mark 1 : 9-11." *S.J.T.*, 8 (1955).
 "S. Mark IV. 1-34." *S.J.T.*, 4 (1951).

W. D. Davies. *Archbishop Carrington's The Primitive Christian Calendar.* The Background of the New Testament and its Eschatology. Ed. W. D. Davies and D. Daube. Cambridge University Press, 1956.

C. H. Dodd. "The Framework of the Gospel Narrative." *E.T.*, 43 (1932) and in *New Testament Studies.* Manchester University Press, 1953.

B. S. Easton. *A Primitive Tradition in Mark.* Studies in Early Christianity. Ed S. J. Case. The Century Co., 1928.

C. F. Evans. "I will go before you into Galilee." *J.T.S.* (n.s.), 5 (1954).

J. C. Fenton. *Paul and Mark.* Studies in the Gospels. Ed. D. E. Nineham. Blackwell, 1955.

M. Glasswell. *The Use of Miracles in the Markan Gospel.* Miracles. Ed. C. F. D. Moule. A. R. Mowbray, 1965.

N. Q. Hamilton. "Resurrection Tradition and the Composition of Mark." *J.B.L.*, 84 (1965).

G. Herbert. "The Resurrection Narrative in St Mark's Gospel." *S.J.T.*, 15 (1962).

L. E. Keck. "Mark 3 : 7-12 and Mark's Christology." *J.B.L.*, 84 (1965).

G. D. Kilpatrick. *The Gentile Mission in Mark and Mark 13. 9-11.* Studies in the Gospels. Ed. D. E. Nineham. Blackwell, 1955.

—— "Mark 13. 9-10." *J.T.S.* (n.s.) 9 (1958).

O. Linton "The Trial of Jesus and the Interpretation of Ps. 110." *N.T.S.* 7 (1961).

I. H. Marshall. "The Synoptic Son of Man Sayings." *N.T.S.*, 12 (1966).

D. E. Nineham. *The Order of Events in St Mark's Gospel.* An Examination of Dr Dodd's Hypothesis. Studies in the Gospels. Ed. D. E. Nineham. Blackwell, 1955.

A. W. Mosley. "Jesus' Audiences in the Gospels of St Mark and St Luke." *N.T.S.*, 10 (1963).

S. Sandmel. "Prolegomena to a Commentary on Mark." *J. B. R.* 31 (1963).

H. Sawyer. "The Marcan Framework." *S.J.T.*, 14 (1961).

A. Shaw. "The Marcan Feeding Miracles." *C.Q.R.*, clxii (1961).

E. F. Seegman. "Teaching in Parables." *C.B.Q.*, 23 (1961).

O. J. F. Seetz. "Praeparatio Evangelica in the Markan Prologue." *J.B.L.*, 82 (1963).

C. W. F. Smith. "No Time for Figs." *J.B.L.*, 79 (1960).

V. Taylor. "The Origin of the Markan Passion Sayings." *N.T.S.* 1 (1954-5).

J. B. Tyson. "The Blindness of the Disciples in Mark." *J.B.L.*, 80 (1961).